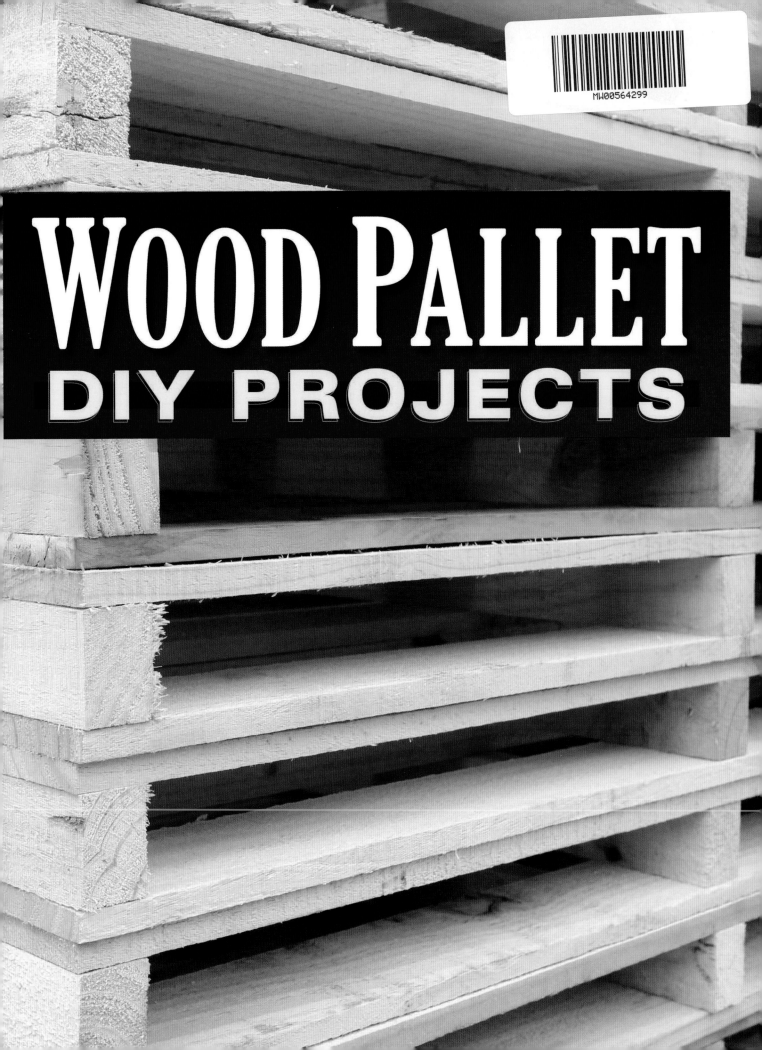

WOOD PALLET
DIY PROJECTS

WOOD PALLET
DIY PROJECTS

20 BUILDING PROJECTS TO ENRICH YOUR HOME, YOUR HEART & YOUR COMMUNITY

Stephen & Diane Fitzberger

FOX CHAPEL
PUBLISHING

Dedication

This book is dedicated first to the One Who met and provided for us every step of the way, our Lord, our Savior, and the Lover of our souls: Jesus.

To our boys and our daughter-in-law who inspire us to stay adventurous and dream big!

To our family and friends who encouraged us in this project…we are grateful!

And finally, to the people and city of Baltimore…you have our heart!

© 2018 by Stephen Fitzberger, Diane Fitzberger, and Fox Chapel Publishing Company, Inc., 903 Square Street, Mount Joy, PA 17552.

Wood Pallet DIY Projects is an original work, first published in 2018 by Fox Chapel Publishing Company, Inc. The patterns contained herein are copyrighted by the author. Readers may make copies of these patterns for personal use. The patterns themselves, however, are not to be duplicated for resale or distribution under any circumstances. Any such copying is a violation of copyright law.

ISBN 978-1-56523-930-2

Library of Congress Cataloging-in-Publication Data

Names: Fitzberger, Stephen, author. | Fitzberger, Diane, author.
Title: Wood pallet DIY projects / Stephen Fitzberger and Diane Fitzberger.
Description: Mount Joy, PA : Fox Chapel Publishing Company, 2018. | Includes
   index.
Identifiers: LCCN 2017059823 | ISBN 9781565239302
Subjects: LCSH: Woodwork--Patterns. | Pallets (Shipping, storage,
   etc.)--Miscellanea. | Salvage (Waste, etc.)
Classification: LCC TT180 .F58 2018 | DDC 684/.08--dc23
LC record available at https://lccn.loc.gov/2017059823

To learn more about the other great books from Fox Chapel Publishing, or to find a retailer near you, call toll-free 800-457-9112 or visit us at *www.FoxChapelPublishing.com*.

We are always looking for talented authors. To submit an idea, please send a brief inquiry to acquisitions@foxchapelpublishing.com.

Printed in China
Fifth printing

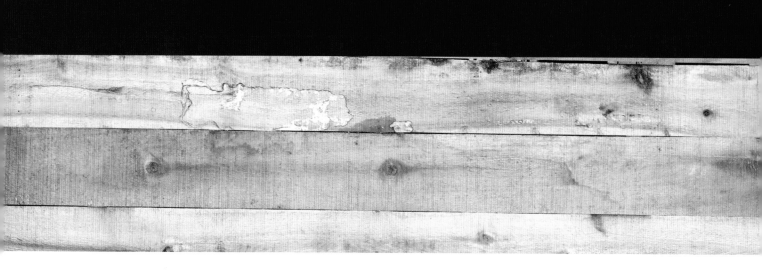

Contents

PROJECTS FOR YOUR YARD & COMMUNITY ... 28

PROJECTS FOR YOUR HOME 72

Reclaimed Wood—Reclaimed Lives

This block is just crying out for beautification. How could you enhance it?

We live in Baltimore, Maryland, and we love our city! We love its personality, its history, and its people. It is a place being filled with hope! Baltimore is a hardworking, no-nonsense kind of town that like most large cities has its struggles but works hard to press through and find the beauty in the ashes. With abandoned lots in the middle of the city, and people sometimes struggling in other ways, we've found that often a bit of attention can help restore both. Here in Baltimore, we found the perfect opportunity to share our skills and offer direction that not only benefits them, but can also help turn forgotten neighborhoods into places of hope and beauty.

We started our company, Abba Woodworks, LLC, few years ago with a desire to be a company that would truly build into the community, no matter how big or how small. We wanted to take the skills we had spent the majority of our lives developing and use them to help others in very practical ways. To create a company that not only made great products but sought to invest in the people and our city on as many levels and in as many ways as possible. To be a place where you could learn new skills or improve on the ones you had. We wanted to establish a place where you could begin to reclaim your life if you had struggled to overcome addiction, homelessness, or just needed an opportunity because your path was different from the norm. A place where you would be welcome and feel cared about, no matter what your skill level. A place where you could be proud of the work of your hands and build up the people you worked with. A place where you might be taking something that would otherwise end up in a landfill and transform it into something beautiful and useful. It sounds a bit utopic, we know, but why not?

Many of the neighborhoods in Baltimore are considered "food deserts," which means that they are a place that doesn't have a local grocery store, so it is difficult to buy fresh fruits and vegetables. We thought, "Why not create a way that you could have a garden, no matter where you lived, a way to have community gardens on any surface?"

"We wanted to establish a place where you could begin to reclaim your life."

Around the same time, we were approached by a good friend who was working with a couple of the elementary schools in the city. He was working as a permacultural-ist and was teaching the children about plants and how they grow. Many of the children had never had a garden and didn't really know where their food came from. They were excited to plant seeds and see how they turned into plants with things that were beautiful and amazing to taste! He wanted to provide gardens for them to plant even more things and to see what they could grow by the end of the semester. He didn't have money to go and buy

Stephen enjoys interacting with the community as a vendor at farmers' markets.

At Abba Woodworks, LLC, people can build a sense of dignity as they build with their hands.

wood and materials for the beds, so he reached out to us to see if we had any ideas or a way to make it happen.

We had learned that the majority of wooden shipping pallets are made with heat-treated wood and were much safer to use for gardens than pressure-treated wood. We also knew that many are discarded after the deliveries arrive, but that they could surely be used for something! So, we started collecting them from businesses around the city and began making raised garden beds. We were so excited to see them harvest their crops and celebrate with an end-of-semester "salad party"!

We decided to continue making the beds and applied to be a vendor at our downtown farmers' market, which had become one of our favorite places to attend on the weekend. The door opened up and we began our journey.

We realized that the pallets were a perfect thing to use because we would not only be upcycling, which is so important in a city like ours, but that they would be the perfect material to work with for our company. They would provide a way to bring someone in at any stage of ability and allow them to grow in whatever skills they chose. Pallets have to be disassembled before you can work with them, so even pulling boards apart and pulling nails is a major part of what needs to happen. If that is all you want to do or are able to do, you are still worth your weight in gold! We start with basic instruction on working with tools and wood and go from there. Teach-

ing everything from how to read the grain and strength of the wood to how to read and use a tape measure. Then we look at what tool is best to use for the job to be accomplished and what is the best way to approach the task at hand. Basic shop safety and use of equipment comes next. We then work with layout, design, and assembly. Some of the men who have worked with us have worked in construction, so they came in with great building and tool skills; we just added some cabinetmaking tips and techniques and they began to make beautiful things.

Sometimes it just takes an open door and the encouragement to walk through it. We were once told that learning how to understand all the markings on a tape measure was a "game changer." Having struggled in math in school, the fractions were intimidating and confusing. Being able to understand what they meant and how to apply them in creating a project was invaluable. Another person told us that just having the opportunity to work with his hands again and make things that would help people had encouraged him to begin dreaming about his life again.

We love what we do and the people we do it with!

For today, we still have our "day" jobs to help cover expenses, so we work with our guys and our company as time allows during our off-hours and weekends. We love being a part of the small business community that, most of the time, is literally on the city streets!

We are vendors at the Baltimore Farmers' Market and Bazaar along with 160 other amazing farmers and vendors on Sundays, right in the heart of the city, just blocks away from City Hall and the Inner Harbor. We are also at the Fells Point Farmers' Market that meets on Saturdays, a few miles east along the water in the town square. Both are markets that set up as the sun is coming up and tear down shortly after lunchtime so that traffic and business continue as usual. They are both major destinations for people in the city and surrounding counties. Our favorite part is talking with our customers and visitors to the city. Our hope is that we are a part of what makes it great!

We are building, and we are growing, as is the hope for our city. We have big dreams for our company and our city, and why not? We know the possibilities are even bigger!

Enriching Your Community

We are all a part of a community of some sort: the community we live in, the community that bonds us by a common interest or passion, and most of all, the community of humankind. Enriching our communities by investing our time and energy not only makes them better, but also adds so much to our own lives. Getting to know people, helping in practical ways, and achieving things that we cannot do on our own is worth any investment we can make.

Many of the products in this book were created with bettering our communities in mind. Building benches and garden beds for a local park area, making products to be used as raffle items for fundraisers, or giving them to area nonprofits to use in their facilities are just a few ideas. You could volunteer your time with a youth organization to show them some basic woodworking skills and make a small project. There are needs everywhere, and it doesn't always take a lot of investment to have a big impact. So, look around and see where you can help. You won't be sorry that you did!

About the Authors

The authors, Stephen and Diane Fitzberger

Stephen has been a journeyman cabinetmaker for more than 30 years and has honed his skills at businesses around Baltimore and in the Washington DC area.

Diane has spent her career in banking, bookkeeping, and accounting. They have both spent more than enough time on the road with their jobs and wanted to come up with something for this next stage of their lives that would not only utilize their skills but would be something close to their hearts: practical help. They hope you enjoy the book!

Creating a better environment while enriching lives.

Let's Get Started!

The best thing about working with wood pallets is that the possibilities are endless! Indoor, outdoor, large, small, rustic, or finished, with a little sweat equity, as they say, "If you can dream it, you can build it." You can create pieces that are truly one of a kind and are designed to fit the space you have with the look you want.

With that being said, the hardest thing about working with pallets is that (1) they require a bit of hard work to disassemble before building your project, and (2) you are working with what you *have* instead of starting with uniformly cut, planed, and sanded pieces of wood.

The payoff, however, is that you can take pride in having created unique pieces that you made by yourself or with a friend, or turned into a family or community project. You are also working with wood that would otherwise end up in a landfill! Good for the environment, good for your community, and good for your creative juices—win, win, win!

The projects covered in this book range from pretty simple to a little more complicated. We will walk you through each one step by step and give you some woodworking tips along the way. Each project has a picture of the finished product, a list of equipment needed, the materials needed, and the start-to-finish instructions with pictures and written descriptions.

Many of the projects use a jigsaw, a chop saw, and a table saw. We have found that when you use all three on a project, it can make the job easier and you end up with a more finished look. We chose the tools that we felt were the most straightforward for each project, but feel free to work with what you are most comfortable with and what fits best in your work space. So, whether you have a nicely equipped workshop or are working in your yard or driveway, you will be able to make amazing pieces that you can be proud of.

If you are an old pro at woodworking, we hope to give you a few new project ideas and a few tips along the way.

> **"You are also working with wood that would otherwise end up in a landfill! Good for the environment, good for your community, and good for your creative juices."**

Instead of uniformly cut, planed, and sanded wood, pallets require you to work with what you have.

And if you are new to woodworking and pallet projects, we hope to introduce you to the tools and equipment you'll be using and explain why one piece of equipment may be better to use than another to accomplish your task. Either way, we hope to encourage and inspire you with some fun projects that can be done in a relatively short amount of time.

Some of the projects will give you the option of using the full width of the pallet or just half of it, depending on your preference or your space available. So know that even if you see a project presented in a certain way, you may be able to make a few adjustments and make it work even better for you!

Relax, have fun, and enjoy the creative process. Even if the piece ends up a little different than you were thinking, it may just add to its one-of-a-kind appeal!

So, if you're ready, let's get started!

Pallets come in a variety of shapes and sizes, each designed according to the product being shipped, the industry they serve, and the country they come from.

Some Pallet Basics

At first glance, most wooden pallets seem the same. On closer inspection, and once you start looking for certain ones for a project, you discover that there are actually several different designs. There are different shapes, sizes, widths, and lengths. They are each designed for the industry they serve, the products they ship, and the country they come from.

You may have heard the terms *pallet* and *skid* used to describe the same wooden frame. Pallets are actually those with slats on both sides, while a skid will only have the slats on one side. They both come in several shapes, sizes, treatments, and colors.

The most common pallet you see is 48" x 40" (122 x 102cm) and is 6 ½" (17cm) tall. This is also the industry

standard wooden pallet for U.S. industry. Some have "stringer" boards with forklift cutouts that create a base for the deck or plank boards, while others use blocks. Some of the longer pallets have stringer boards with wooden feet. While this is the most common, you can definitely find a wide variety of pallets with the parts you want to complete a project.

The most important thing to do is to make sure that the pallets you are working with are safe. You never want to work with a pallet that has liquid-like stains, sticky substances, or odors. Painted pallets can be fine to work with, but you would not want to use them for planting vegetables or using as a serving tray. Pallets can be sanded, but you don't want to work with anything that has been chemically treated or saturated with an unknown substance.

The majority of pallets you will find will have a stamp on one of the side pieces. Don't use a pallet without a stamp. The two main things to look for on a pallet stamp are the International Plant Protection Convention (IPPC) logo that will be printed beside a wheat symbol and the "HT" (heat treated) initials. These stamps mean that the pallet has met agency standards to travel internationally and has been made of materials that will not carry invasive insects or plant diseases. The HT stamp means that the pallet has been heat treated and not chemically treated. "MB" (Methyl Bromide) is a stamp that means the pallet has been treated chemically and is not safe to use. They have been banned, but you could still come across one that has been in storage for a long time. The most important thing is to be safe, so always look for these symbols. Information about what a particular stamp means may be found online.

Where do you find pallets?

We're going to warn you up front that when you start thinking about pallet projects, you are going to start seeing pallets *everywhere*! You never knew that they were hiding in plain sight! You'll see them behind local businesses, stacked beside dumpsters, riding down the road in the back of a pick-up truck or a flatbed, and even in your neighbor's driveway. A lot of businesses are starting to reuse their pallets, but there are still quite a few that would be happy for you to take a few home with you. You always want to ask before taking, just in case.

The type of business will determine the type of pallets they use. The long pallets tend to be found at manufacturing companies. Most offices, stores, and garden or landscaping businesses have pallets that are around 4" (10cm) tall.

Pallets can also be bought new, so choose what you are most comfortable with, and start planning your projects!

Label	Meaning
HT	Heat treated
KD	Kiln dried
MB	Methyl bromide treated
DB	Debarked
S-P-F	Contains spruce, pine, or fir components

Avoid pallets stamped with "MB," for these have been chemically treated and are not safe to use.

Color Variations

When wood pallets are new, they are very light or even blonde. As they age, they naturally warm up in color from the sunlight and oxygen, much as your wood floors do over time. When left outdoors in all of the elements, the untreated wood will continue to change, or oxidize (become gray). You can use this to your advantage when designing your projects.

It is a great idea to have a couple of pallets to work with on any project. This will allow you to pick and choose the boards you like and make up for any broken pieces. It will also enable you to choose a couple of pallets of various ages, adding another dimension. You can create a piece with mostly oxidized wood by leaving as many uncut surfaces as possible and then use a stain or leather polish to "age" the freshly cut edges.

If you have the time and space available, you can leave a few pallets outside and let them age naturally in the heat and rain of the summer and the cold and snow of the winter.

Left: Exposure from sunlight and oxygen will change the color of untreated wood from blonde to gray.

Opposite: To attain a specific color, a stain or leather polish may be used if you don't have time to age the wood naturally.

Embracing the "Imperfections"

Pallet wood tends to have a lot of personality! Variations include different colors and distinctive grain marks, nail and knot holes, or rough or broken edges. Embracing the uniqueness can add a lot to your project. Incorporating these details can be the focal point or just an added element, so choose the layout of your project based on what you want to highlight. Our favorite pieces often include wood that at first glance would end up in the scrap pile, but when we choose to embrace the "imperfection," it made the project so much better.

Keep this in mind when you are choosing the pallets for your project. This is another reason that it is great to have a few pallets to work with to mix and match your wood. Get creative! Put pieces together that you wouldn't necessarily choose to go together and see what sparks your artistic eye. So much of the fun of working with pallet wood is that no two projects are exactly the same, and many times the contrast is what sets it apart as a true original and keepsake. So get those creative juices flowing, and you might just amaze yourself at how truly talented you are!

Colors, grain marks, knot holes, and rough edges offer variety to your wood selection. Don't be afraid to combine them!

Paints, rubs, and finishes not only make the wood more vibrant; they also protect the wood.

Paints, Stains & Finishes

You really have your choice when it comes to finishing wooden pallet projects. Since most pallets found in the United States are made from southern white pine and oak, they perform well with a wide variety of finishes. Both woods also have nice grain marks that become more vibrant with stains and oils. The pop of color you can add with paint is always a fun option. Paints, rubs, and finishes also add an extra layer of protection to the wood and will last for years. So get creative! New finishing products, processes, and techniques are coming out all the time, so have fun, experiment, and explore! Be sure to follow the manufacturer's instructions and apply the finish in a safe area, and be prepared to amaze yourself!

Sweat the Small Stuff

Well, you don't actually have to sweat, but know that paying attention to little details can add a lot to your project!

Making sure that your edges are sanded, your ends are flush, and your joints are tight will add to the overall finished look. It will also add strength and support to each piece.

No detail is too small to overlook, so pay attention to the little details as you build. You will be happy with the result!

Use Everything

One of the best features of working with wood pallets is that you can use the entire pallet for a new use. Set aside any unused planks and stringer boards for another project, and cut up any small or broken pieces to use for kindling for your fire pit. The wood is well dried so it works great as a fire starter. We actually bundle the pieces together in small batches and stack them for easy use.

Get creative with the nails! Check with a local art school or artist to see if they would like the twisted and aged nails for their projects. We have several artists in our area who love the character they add to their pieces.

There may be other uses for your "scraps," so think outside the box and use everything you can!

Save your scraps of wood, and even used nails, and let your imagination find a use for them.

Tools of the Trade

There are many tools and pieces of equipment to choose from when you are building wood projects. Some are large, some small, some stationary, and some portable. What you choose to use can depend on a lot of things, from your space and your budget to what you are most comfortable using. The space you have to work in can dictate quite a bit. Do you have the ability to set up a shop and leave things in place? Or do you need to set things up and then hang them up or store them out of the way after you use them? Do you prefer using hand tools and the flexibility they provide instead of stationary ones? What is your budget? Many stores will allow you to rent equipment for the day or weekend if you are just working on a single project. You may even have a friend or family member who will loan you a tool that they have. There are many possibilities, but you do want to think about what works best for you before you make a purchase.

Here is a list and a description of the tools we chose to use throughout the book. Some of the pieces of equipment can be used for a few different tasks, but we chose to highlight the ones we felt would work best in the setting shown. Again, always use what you are most comfortable with. As with most things in life, there is more than one way to do something.

PORTABLE TABLE SAW

This is an electric saw with one round, 10" stationary blade that comes up through the middle of the table. The blade height and angle can be adjusted. It has an adjustable metal rip fence on one side of the blade. Some models will allow you to place the fence on either side, to use what works best for you. You adjust the fence for the width of your cut. It will provide you with a clean, uniform edge for your pieces. It also comes with a miter gauge that will allow you to cut angles and crosscut pieces. You are never to use the miter gauge and rip fence at the same time for safety reasons. When you are cutting narrow pieces, it is best to use a "push stick" to keep your fingers away from the blade. We used this mostly with the rip fence to ensure consistently clean-cut edges.

PORTABLE CHOP SAW

This is an electric saw with one 10" stationary blade on a hinged arm that is pulled down to "chop" through a piece of wood that is held perpendicular on the base. It will produce a clean, thorough cut. It also has an adjustable base that can be set at a range of angles, from 90 to 52 degrees, to produce crisp, angled cuts. It can be set up with a fence for longer pieces. You can also set up a "stop" for multiple pieces of the same length. We used this in a variety of ways with most of the projects.

WOODEN FENCE

A wooden fence consists of two pieces of wood joined together in an L shape to produce an attachable piece that aids in the process of cutting with the chop saw. It is mainly used to cut longer pieces and/or multiple similar cuts. A "stop" block can be attached to allow you to cut the same length without measuring every time. It is attached to the chop saw with screws through the metal brackets on the back of the saw, which ensures a secure fit. You can add a vertical board or "leg" to the fence for added support with longer boards. You can make your own fence with scrap wood. They are usually 8 to 12 feet (2–4m), depending on what you are intending to make.

PORTABLE JIGSAW

This is an electric or battery-operated reciprocating handsaw with a thin single metal blade of various lengths that makes a quick cut and was designed to give you the ability to cut curves and shapes. The blades come in a few different designs to cut different materials, based on what you are working with. There are blades designed for cutting wood, plastic, and metal. This is a great, lightweight saw to use for its mobility and versatility. The only drawback is that it does not always produce a clean edge. You may want to either trim the ends with a table or chop saw, or sand them well. We used this saw in most of our projects because of its ability to quickly disassemble the pallets in a safe way.

SAWZALL®

This is also an electric or battery-operated reciprocating handsaw with a thin, single metal blade. Different blades can be purchased as well to cut the material you are working with. The main difference between a jigsaw and a Sawzall is the ability of the Sawzall to cut heavier materials. While the jigsaw will allow you to make delicate, curved cuts, the Sawzall will give you a little more weight behind your cut. It is great for cutting through nails as well as wood and plastic. We used this saw to cut through joints of some pallets and to remove the "feet" off the pallets with twisted metal nails.

PORTABLE HAND DRILL

This is an electric or battery-operated, handheld device that will allow you to drill a hole into a piece of wood. It is great to use because it makes a quick, clean hole that can help prevent the wood from splitting. This will keep the wood stronger and your holes more uniform, allowing the nails or screws to fit more securely. You can purchase different sizes of drill bits to fit your need. You can also make your own small bit by cutting the head off of a brad with end nippers and fitting the brad into the chuck.

PORTABLE SCREW GUN

This is an electric or battery-operated, handheld device that will allow you to insert and tighten screws quickly and easily. It will help you ensure that pieces are secure and well joined, creating stronger joints.

HANDHELD BELT SANDER

This is an electric device that allows you to smooth out rough material with an abrasive belt. Belts with different grits can be used to achieve the smoothness you desire. Because of its design, it is a great tool to use to smooth a surface quickly with minimum effort. Its strength can damage your material if you do not use it with a gentle, uniform motion. It takes a little practice to use a belt sander well, but it is worth the effort to accomplish your task. We used this sander on the projects with large surface areas.

GRIT NUMBERS

The number on the sandpaper signifies the number of stones (those gritty bumps) within a 1" x 1" (2.5 x 2.5cm) area. The larger the number, the finer the sandpaper: finer sandpaper produces a smoother finish.

HANDHELD ORBITAL SANDER

This is an electric device that allows you to quickly sand a surface to provide a finer finish. It has removable sanding disks with different grits to achieve the smoothness you desire. It moves in an orbital, or egg-shaped, motion that allows it to cover an area with fewer marks. You will often use this sander after a belt sander has done the hard work to create a more polished look. We typically used it on the corners and edges that would be handled the most. We also used it on the tabletops and bench surfaces.

SAWHORSES

These are structures that are used to support items at a height that is easier to work from. They can be purchased or made and are generally made of plastic or wood. Most sawhorses are a set height of 24" to 38" (61–97cm), but they do make adjustable ones, and you can also make your own to the height you want. You can place a piece of equipment or the project you are working on directly on the sawhorses.

PARTICLEBOARD OR PLYWOOD "TABLE"

This is a piece of plywood or particleboard that is used to create a stable work surface on top of your sawhorses. This creates a portable work surface that is great for drilling, assembling, and finishing.

AIR-POWERED TOOLS

When using air-powered tools, it is best to buy a package deal that will come with a compressor with an air hose and a number of pneumatic fasteners (usually three). These often include a staple gun, a brad gun, and a finish nail gun. *Always wear safety glasses when using these tools.*

LAYOUT TOOLS

These are hand tools that help you measure and mark your pieces. They include a speed square, a combination square, framing square, chalk line, and a measuring tape. The speed, combination, and framing squares have a solid edge that is great to use to mark a wide area. They will also help you to establish a 90-degree angle when held flush with the side of your board. The chalk line can be used to mark a straight line for a long cut. The measuring tape is flexible and long enough that it can be used for just about everything. Use it to mark your pieces, to measure the space for your project, and to make sure your heights, lengths, and widths are correct.

TOOLS TO DISASSEMBLE THE PALLETS

These are hand tools that will help you disassemble or take apart the wood pallets. They include a hammer, cold chisel, channel locks, vice grips, a flat bar, fence pliers, and lineman's pliers. The hammer, cold chisel, and flat bar will help you separate the wood. The channel locks, vice grips, fence pliers, and lineman's pliers are all used to pull the nails. Each tool has its own features, so use the one that works best for the situation. The cold chisels will need to be sharpened from time to time with the metal file.

CLAMPS

Clamps come in a variety of shapes, sizes, and material. Most are made of metal or plastic. They are designed for the size and the amount of pressure needed to hold pieces in place. Choose what works best for the job at hand, making sure to come back and check that they are holding in place and applying the amount of pressure you need. Switch out if necessary.

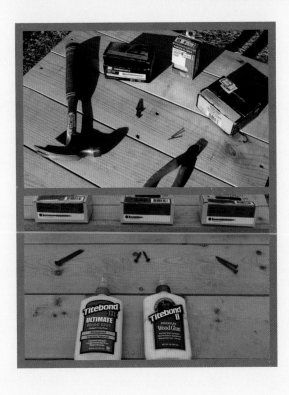

WOOD GLUE, BRADS, NAILS, SCREWS, AND END NIPPERS

These items are used to assemble your project. It is best, in most cases, to use a thin line of wood glue on your project to avoid the glue from squeezing out from between the surfaces. You can use a zig-zag pattern to cover a large area. When you apply glue to a piece that will then get reinforced with a brad or nail, you don't need to wait for the glue to dry. The glue will dry holding everything in place. The end nippers can be used to create a drill bit for predrilling with a brad, by cutting the head off the brad and placing the brad in the chuck. Brads are best to use with small projects and when you want them to stay somewhat hidden. Larger common nails are best to use when more support is needed or when you want to create a certain look. We used coated deck screws on most of the projects that required screws. We prefer using them for their durability and the versatility with outdoor and indoor projects.

Because of the tools involved, working with wood requires special attention to safety.

Safety: First, Last & Middle

It almost goes without saying that when working with power tools and saws, safety is of the utmost importance! No matter how long you have worked with them, because things can happen so quickly, it is best to establish some general rules of practice to ensure a safe environment. Here are a few things to remember as you work.

1. **Wear safety glasses or goggles.** Safety glasses will not only protect your eyes from sawdust, they will keep your eyes safe from any flying debris. Bifocal safety glasses are also available, which will help you see the fine details.

2. **Tie your hair out of the way, if necessary.** Be sure to keep your hair out of your eyes and the length away any machinery so it doesn't get caught.

3. **Keep sleeves above your elbow, tuck any loose clothing in, and remove any dangling jewelry.** This is a general rule in most woodshops and is a good rule to follow in your work space. Doing all you can to keep any fabric or jewelry from getting damaged or caught in the equipment and causing you harm is always a good idea.

4. **Work in an area with good lighting and ventilation.** This is one of the most important safety rules. Good lighting and good ventilation will not only keep you safe but could save your life.

5. **Make sure that your power tools are in good working order, with all cords and switches secure.** Double check that the motor is running smoothly without any lapse in power or sparks. Check the cords for any fraying or splitting, and make sure that they are properly attached to the tool and their plug. Make sure that the switches are working correctly and are not loose. When using a power tool, make sure its plug is held securely held in the outlet.

6. **Wear ear plugs or earmuffs.** These are a good idea to protect your hearing from the volume and constant sound of the power tools and saws. They will keep the noise levels to a minimum while still allowing you to hear.

7. **Wear gloves and masks when working with stains and toxic glues.** This will protect your skin, eyes, and respiratory system from anything harmful. Be sure to safely dispose of the gloves and masks, and safely store any unused stain or glue out of the reach of children and animals.

8. **Be careful to keep all power cords and extension cords out of the way.** Be aware of the cords while the tool is in use, being careful not to have them where they can be tripped over, cut, or tangled. Make sure that any connection is tight.

9. **Work on stable work surfaces.** Making sure that the surfaces are level and secure can keep the tools and equipment from tipping or shifting. This can prevent both injuries and errors in the work.

10. **Be sure to clean up any nails, screws, or any other sharp objects.** Making sure your work area is safe to walk in is critical. You will not only save you from an unnecessary injury, but you will be able to properly dispose of the materials and save any unused pieces.

11. **Make sure your tools are turned off and stored in safe, secure places.** Be sure to turn off the power, unplug the cords, and keep your tools in a location where they will not fall and break or be tripped over. Keep them locked away and out of the reach of children, if necessary.

12. **Be mindful of any distractions.** Stay alert to your surroundings and do your best to avoid any unnecessary interruptions.

Developing your own safety routines and habits will create the best working environment. You may even want to come up with your own safety checklist to keep on hand. Most accidents happen when someone is new to a tool or has been working with them for so long that they become too casual with their safety practices. Make sure to read instructions thoroughly when working with a new tool. Enjoy learning new techniques and processes, and always stay curious!

Always protect yourself when working with wood.

PROJECTS FOR YOUR YARD & COMMUNITY

Raised Garden Bed

45" x 15" x 15" (114 x 38 x 38cm)

This project is our absolute favorite! Not only is it a beautiful way to organize and add character and design to your outdoor space, but you can also use it to feed your family, your community and those in need! We have friends that plant several gardens with the sole purpose of growing and donating the produce to families in the area. They get to share the care and responsibility of tending the gardens while spending time together for a worthy cause. You could also coordinate a community garden with each family building their own bed the size and shape they want and then sharing the bounty!

A raised garden bed by its design is easier on your back. And by having the soil contained above the ground, the added warmth allows it to grow just about anything. We designed this box in a way that the dimensions can be changed to make larger or smaller beds and can be adjusted to create a square bed as well, whatever you want for your unique space. The largest boxes we have made are a square 6' x 6' (2 x 2m) and a rectangular 12' x 30" (4 x 9m), and the smallest boxes we make are 15" x 15" x 15" (38 x 38 x 38cm).

We love the look and function of several different beds arranged together. When you have a plant that will spread and that likes to take over, like mint, it is nice to be able to contain it in its own space. Some plants do better growing in their own space, while others thrive alongside other varieties.

These beds are designed without a bottom because they do just fine set on top of the ground or even on a brick or cement patio. A bottom can be added if you want to place it on a deck by adding a layer of boards cut to size along the bottom edge and securing with narrow boarder pieces. Spacing the boards a little apart or drilling drain holes will provide drainage. You can line the bed with garden felt if you like. We have found that they do fine either way, so it is whatever you are most comfortable with.

BEST SIZE/SHAPE PALLET TO USE

31" x 144" (79 x 366cm) marked with HT and a wheat stamp—this will ensure that the beds are safe for vegetables. Use a second pallet with different coloring for the vertical side pieces if you want to achieve a multi-colored look. Make sure the plank thickness is similar and cut to size and length to match.

We use this size pallet for the length of the side rails. Using one continuous piece as a side frame provides strength and stability and can be adjusted to the size bed you want.

TOOLS

- Jigsaw
- Tape measure
- Sawzall® with metal cutting blade
- Hammer
- Chop saw with fence
- Chisel
- Nail gun
- Nail punch
- Screw gun
- Chalk line
- Sawhorses
- Channel locks
- Adjustable clamps
- Bucket for discarded nails

MATERIALS

- 1 pallet, 31" x 144" (2 if color variation is desired)
- 2" (50mm) nails
- 1" (25mm) nails or staples
- 2 ½" (60mm) deck screws
- 50 grit sandpaper
- 1 ¼" (30mm) deck screws

1. Lay the pallet on a level surface. Begin by marking the pallet to prepare for the cuts you will need to make. Measure and mark an X at 15½" (40cm) (or center) every couple of plank boards. These will become the vertical side pieces.

2. Mark a second X on the plank boards that line up with the "feet." These pieces will be discarded or used for other projects, as they have an extra piece attached for the stability of the shipping pallet that is not necessary for the raised bed.

3. Use a jigsaw to cut the center of each plank without a double X.

4. Remove each cut piece.

5. Place in a pile for easy accessibility when assembling.

6. Place the pallet on sawhorses to create a stable work surface. Use the jigsaw to cut the plank boards with the double X along the inside stringer rail.

7. Knock off the remaining pieces with a hammer and set aside.

8. Flip the stringer board over. Hammer the nails back through the board and remove with the claw end of the hammer, or channel locks if the nail is broken.

9. Secure the stringer board to the sawhorses with the clamps to remove the feet.

10. Knock the feet loose with a hammer to create a gap, then pry the feet away from the board with the chisel and hammer.

11. Cut through the twisted nails with the Sawzall.

12. Hammer the nails back through the board and remove. Use a nail punch to push the shorter nails through, if necessary. Set up a fence for the chop saw to create the garden bed rails. See the Tools of the Trade section at the beginning of the book for a description and instructions on how to make your own fence. Trim a straight edge on the end of the first piece. This will give a clean and uniform cut that will give the bed smooth, well-fit edges.

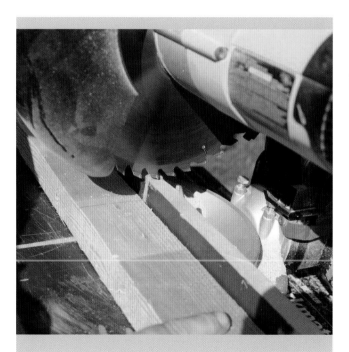

13. Measure, mark, and cut two 45" (114cm) pieces and two 15" (38cm) pieces from each stringer board.

14. Set up a stop on the chop saw to cut 15" (38cm) pieces.

15. Cut four 15" (38cm) pieces. Leave the stop in place to create the vertical pieces for the sides of the garden bed after building the frame.

16. Start building the frame by attaching the end and side pieces to create an L. Use two 2" (50mm) nails to attach the pieces.

17. Repeat with the other end and side.

18. Fit the two Ls together to create the first frame.

19. Predrill two holes in each end.

20. Place the 2½" (60mm) deck screws in to secure.

21. Repeat for the second frame.

22. Remove the nails from the vertical boards by hammering back through and removing with the claw end of the hammer.

23. Trim and cut each vertical piece to 15" (38cm) using the chop saw. This, again, will create uniform pieces that provide a smooth, well-fit edge.

24. Place a vertical piece in each corner and put two nails or staples at the top and two at the bottom of each board to secure them to the frame.

25. Predrill a hole at the center top and bottom of each board. Predrilling will keep the board from splitting and provide added stability for the screw.

26. Place a 1¼" (30mm) screw in to secure it to the frame. Place a common nail at the top and bottom in between the boards as a spacer.

27. Predrill and screw the next board in place and continue the process, moving the spacer nails until the bed is complete. Trim any pieces in width to fit as necessary.

28. Sand the top and bottom rails. Paint, stain, or clear coat only the outside, if planting vegetables. This prevents any toxins from getting into the soil. You can use a layer of beeswax on the inside if desired. If you are planting flowers or other plants, you can finish the entire box, or leave it natural. For best results, start with a layer of gravel, then straw for drain fields, then your soil mixture. You are ready to plant!

Vertical Herb Garden

What a great way to showcase your herbs and summer flowers! This vertical herb garden adds function, dimension, and beauty to your outdoor space!

It can be used on a deck, bricked patio, or paved area. The vertical design makes planting and maintenance easy on your back and allows you to display both herbs and flowers or all your favorites of one. It is strong and sturdy and will not tip over on its own.

We used chalkboard paint to add a message and label the herbs. It will also look great painted all one color, painted with your own design, or stained to match your décor.

You can make a few and add an artistic and architectural aspect to your garden space!

BEST SIZE/SHAPE PALLET TO USE

2 – 40" x 48" (102 x 122cm) with 5 plank boards on the underside of the pallet, with 2 larger boards on top and bottom; 1 – 31" x 47" (79 x 120cm) block pallet with ¾" (2cm) plank boards

TOOLS

- Table saw
- Staple gun
- Flat bar or pry bar
- Sawhorses or a stable surface
- Hammer
- Jigsaw
- Wooden block
- Portable drill

MATERIALS

- 2 pallets, 48" x 40", with forklift cutouts
- #4 – 1 ½" (40mm) common nails
- Socket wrench
- Chalkboard paint
- 4 – ¼" x 2 ½" (6 x 60mm) carriage bolts
- Gravel for drainage
- Small paint roller
- Clear coat or colored paint
- ¼" (6mm) washer, lock washer & bolt
- Primer

1. Mark an X on the underside of the boards you want to remove. These will be the ones that do not line up with the sections you want to plant in.

2. Lay the pallet on the sawhorses with the forklift cutouts facing up. Take a block and then hammer the extra boards loose from the frame.

3. Turn the pallet over and remove the boards with the flat bar and then remove the nails.

4. Take the block pallet and remove 4 boards with a hammer and flat bar. We are using these pieces for the base of each planter shelf because the thicker board will create more stability and will allow for more weight.

5. Choose which end you will use for the top and lay the pallet on a stable surface. Secure any board that needs a bit more stability with the staple gun. Measure width and length to the center stringer board and cut baseboards to fit using the table saw.

6. Dry fit and make any adjustment cuts. When trimming small pieces on the table saw, always use a push stick for safety.

7. Hammer the bases into place.

8. Hammer 3 nails into each section along the base line on both sides of the pallet.

9. Cut the top plank boards away from the stringer board on your second pallet to create the feet. Save the pieces for another project.

10. Knock the excess pieces off with a hammer and remove the nails, using vice grips if needed.

11. Measure the shortest edge on the foot piece.

12. Measure and mark the other side with a speed square. Repeat on the other end.

13. Use the jigsaw to cut the pieces to create 2 matching feet.

14. Stand the garden up on a level, stable surface. Place two even boards underneath and line up the feet on each end.

15. Center each foot and use a nail to secure to the frame. Place a second nail below the first one.

16. Adjust the pieces, making sure the planter is vertical and the feet are lined up properly and are stable. Predrill a hole on each side of the nails.

17. Replace with the carriage bolt assembly. Secure with a wrench.

18. Apply the primer and chalkboard paint according to the manufacturer's instructions.

19. Apply the clear coat to the unpainted surfaces. When dry, place a layer of gravel in the bottom of each section. You're ready to plant! Mark your herbs and flowers or write a message for all to enjoy!

Serving/ Grilling/Rain Barrel Table

As you can tell from its title, this project is great because the table is just so versatile! It is sturdy and portable and can be used outdoors, indoors, or both.

You can use it as a side table while you are grilling or a serving table. Or set the top boards a little wider apart and use it as a table to elevate your rain water barrel. It is the perfect size for a tea party or an after-noon of crafts with your little loves.

It looks great with paint or stain as well as left natural, so do what works best for you. We have even made a few with the blue pallets for a really fun look.

TOOLS	MATERIALS
• Jigsaw	• 1 pallet, 30"
• Portable drill	or 36" x 144"
• Flat bar	• Wood glue
• Hammer	• 50 grit sandpaper
• Table saw	• 1 ½" (40mm) brads
• Tape measure	• 1 ¼" (30mm)
• Brad gun (optional)	deck screws
• Channel locks	
• Chop saw	

BEST SIZE/SHAPE PALLET TO USE

144" (366cm) long

1. Starting at the second plank board, cut along the inside rail of each stringer board, leaving the center and end boards attached. Repeat on other side.

2. Put pressure on one end of the plank board and use a flat bar to remove each board. Work in the direction of the grain instead of from the side to prevent splitting the piece.

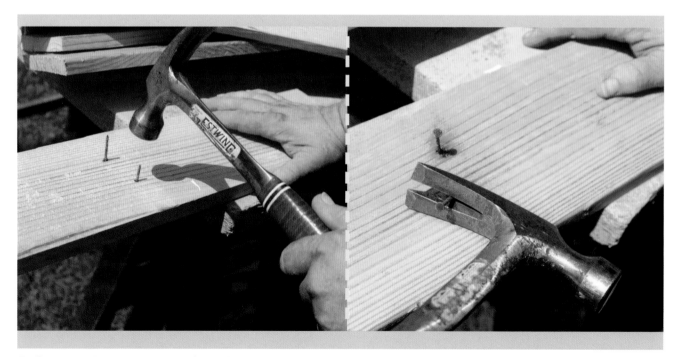

3. Remove the end boards with a jigsaw, leaving the center board in place until you have removed the end boards from each side. Remove the center board. Set the stringer boards aside to use for another project. (See the "Honey" Bench project on page 66.) Remove the nails from each board by hammering the nails back through and removing with the claw end. Use channel locks or vice grips to remove any broken nails.

4. Set aside the pieces you want to use for the top of the table, facing any curvature in the surface downward, enough to measure 25" (64cm) across. Select 4 boards to use as the legs. Trim the shortest piece with a table saw to create clean edges and cut the remaining 3 to match.

5. Cut each piece down the center of the width. Place a thin line of glue down the center of the edge and attach the other piece to form an L. Secure with 5 or 6 brads using a brad gun or predrill and use a hammer and brad, keeping the edges flush. Repeat with the remaining 3 legs. Sand the outside edges.

6. Trim the top edge of each leg with a chop saw and cut to 24" (60cm).

7. Select 4 boards to use for the frame. Trim the shortest piece with a table saw to create clean edges. Cut the remaining 3 to match and then cut down the center width just as you did for the legs. Using the chop saw, trim the top edge of each piece and cut 2 to 24" (60cm) and 2 to 22½" (57cm). To create the upper frame, predrill and screw two 1¼" (30mm) deck screws into each corner. Repeat to create lower frame. We are not using glue here to allow for movement in the table.

8. Hold the top edge of the leg flush with the top edge of the frame. (This will become the base for the tabletop.) Use a staple gun or brads to secure the leg in place. Repeat on each top corner.

9. Take a scrap piece of wood and cut a 12" (30cm) spacer to position the lower frame. Use a clamp to hold in place, and use a staple gun to secure to the frame. Repeat with the remaining corners.

10. Predrill and place 4 screws into each corner to secure.

11. Take the pieces you set aside for the tabletop and use the table saw to trim the sides to create smooth edges. Dry fit your pieces to create the look you desire. Cut a clean edge on each board and cut to 24" (60cm) length. Put back in order and then sand each inner edge before attaching to the frame. Position the first board allowing for a ½" (12mm) overhang and secure with a staple gun.

12. Use a nail as a spacer on each end and secure the remaining boards.

13. Predrill a hole in the center of each board and replace with a screw to secure to the frame.

14. Sand the top and edges.

15. Finish as desired and you are ready to use!

Utensil Caddy

This is a great project that can help you get the party started! We can all use some help staying organized when we have people over, and this utensil caddy is an awesome way to do it. It can be made casual or dressed up a bit. You can even paint it with your favorite sports team colors and pull it out on game day!

It is designed to fit four 18 oz. party cups (one for each group of utensils and a stack of cups) and a supply of napkins; or three 1-quart mason jars, a supply of napkins, and a stack of cups. We used standard drawer pulls for the side handles and trimmed the ends of the mounting screws. It looks great painted, stained, or left natural.

BEST SIZE/SHAPE PALLET TO USE

Any

TOOLS

- Jigsaw
- Brad gun
- Table saw
- Lineman pliers
- Chop saw
- Portable drill

MATERIALS

- 1 pallet, 40" x 40" or 40" x 48" (doesn't really matter because you are cutting pieces to size)
- 1 ½" (40mm) brads
- Paint, stain, or clear coat (optional)
- 80 grit sandpaper
- Drawer handles

1. Cut 8 plank boards away from the stringer board using the jigsaw.

2. Trim one side of each piece using the table saw. Set the fence to 3 ¼" (6mm) width.

3. Flip the boards over and cut the other edge.

4. Cut 2 pieces to 7½" (19cm) length and 2 pieces to 9¾" (25cm) length using the chop saw.

5. Attach a 9¾" (25cm) piece to a 7½" (19cm) piece with 3 brads using the brad gun.

6. Repeat with the other two pieces and attach, creating a box.

7. Trim the next 3 pieces to 3" (76mm) width with the table saw and 9¾" (25cm) length using the chop saw. Dry fit the pieces and trim to fit.

8. Secure each board with 3 brads at each end.

9. Sand the rough edges and finish as you like. Determine the placement of the handles, and mark. Drill holes and attach, trimming the ends if necessary with lineman pliers. You're ready for your next party!

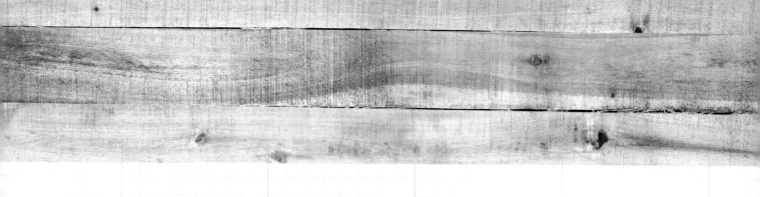

Deck Rail Garden Box

This wonderful garden box will bring a lot of beauty to your deck area with flowering plants or herbs. You can make one or many to fill your outdoor space. The design allows it to sit securely on your deck rail but stay portable enough to relocate it any time you want.

An amazing lady we know from the local farmers' market told us that she created her own relaxing oasis by lining her deck rail with these boxes filled with her favorite fragrant flowers and herbs. She looks forward to coming home each evening and unwinding.

The instructions are designed to fit a standard 5 ½" (14cm) deck rail and a 30" (76cm) liner. The dimensions can be adjusted to fit, if you need a different width and length.

Pallets with wide plank boards work best with this project because of the base and sides. You can use two boards side by side for the base if you can't find the width you need. They may need to be trimmed to fit your overall size.

This is a great project to do with family members or friends to create a unique design statement. The box can be stained, painted, or clear coated. If you are planting herbs, it is best to finish only the outside. This will prevent any chemicals from getting into your soil and your edible herbs.

The wood can also be left unfinished and will naturally oxidize (become gray) with exposure to the sun and rain. You can gently pressure wash it each season to restore the light color.

So make your flower selections and start relaxing!

BEST SIZE/SHAPE PALLET TO USE

Any with wide plank boards

TOOLS
- Portable jigsaw
- Hammer
- End nippers
- Portable drill
- Flat bar
- Table saw
- Speed square
- Tape measure

MATERIALS
- 1 pallet, any size, with wide boards
- 30" x 5 ½" x 5" (76 x 14 x 13cm) window box liner (standard size)
- Wood glue
- 1 ¼" (30mm) brads

1. Cut both ends along the inside edge of the widest 2 plank boards with the jigsaw.

2. Put pressure on one end of the board and use the flat bar to remove the boards from the pallet. Place the flat bar horizontal (with the grain) alongside the board to remove it. Holding it vertical (along the center stringer board) can cause the board to split.

3. Cut one of the narrower boards. Hammer the nails back through the boards and remove.

4. Align the speed square with the bottom edge of the first board and use a pencil to mark a line for a clean edge cut.

5. Measure to 6" (15cm), mark, and cut on the table saw. Repeat. This will become the 2 end pieces.

6. Measure, mark, and cut a piece to 26" (66cm); this is the base piece. Start assembling by building the base first. Use the end nippers to cut the end off of a brad and place it into the drill chuck to predrill holes. Predrilling prevents the boards from splitting and creates a more finished look. Set aside.

7. Place a thin line of glue along the base end, leaving a ½" (12mm) boarder on each dge to allow the glue to spread. Hold 1 side piece flush with the base creating an L. Place any curvature to the inside. Drill 3 holes along the bottom edge and hammer brads into place to attach the pieces. You do not need to let the glue dry. Repeat with the other end.

8. Measure the side length of the box, mark, and cut a side piece to length. Repeat for the other side.

9. Dry fit the side piece measuring 1½" (40mm) beyond bottom edge. This will create the lip that will straddle the deck rail.

10. Apply glue along the side and bottom edges.

11. Hold the pieces in place and predrill 2 holes on each vertical end, then hammer in the brads. Drill 5 holes along the horizontal edge and hammer in the brads. Repeat on other side.

12. Place the liner in the box and measure from the base to the top edge of the box.

13. Adjust the table saw fence and cut the side pieces to the proper width. Hold the piece flush to one end, measure, and mark. Cut to length.

14. Remove the liner and attach with glue and brads as before. Sand any rough edges. Apply the finish you desire. You are ready to plant!

"Honey" Bench

While we may not go so far as to call our little bench a throne, we do have to admit that you might feel pretty regal sitting on it.

We call this our "honey" bench because it is short and sweet and there is only room enough for two! It is just the right size to enjoy a good book under a tree on a sunny day or a relaxing evening with a group of friends around a fire pit enjoying a glass of wine or some s'mores.

A dear friend of ours donated one to a local senior dog sanctuary where she is a volunteer, in remembrance of a sweet pup she lost. It provides a great place for the volunteers to rest as they spend some outdoor time with the "residents"—such an honor.

It is a versatile bench that is great to use outdoors or inside! Because it is both portable and sturdy, it is a piece that can be used just about anywhere. It would be great around a dining room table or in a mud room or entranceway. We even have a couple who uses it as a coffee table. They were relocating out of state and wanted to take a "piece of Baltimore" with them; it made our hearts happy to oblige!

It is made with the support rails of a large pallet, which gives it its extra support and only requires a little sanding since the rails tend to be smoother than the surface boards. Construction is fairly simple, and you can use the pallet deck boards for other projects.

We chose to use decking screws because of their strength and ability to withstand the elements if used outside. You can paint it or leave it natural. You could even have wedding guests sign it with a marker, clear coat it, and give it to the happy couple as keepsake—it is a "honey bench" after all!

If you have several little "honeys" and need a longer bench, you can use rails that are longer in length and add center legs for support.

BEST SIZE/SHAPE PALLET TO USE

144" (366cm) long

TOOLS

- Jigsaw
- Vice grips
- Small bar clamp
- Chop saw with fence
- Flat bar
- Nail gun
- Hammer
- Sawhorses
- Power drill
- Screw gun

MATERIALS

- 1 pallet, 30" or 36" x 144"
- 50 or 80 grit sandpaper
- 2 ½" (60mm) deck screws

1. This project uses the pallet stringer boards that were left over from the Serving Table project. If you are only making the Honey Bench, follow the Serving Table instructions to this point and set the boards aside for another project. Using the jigsaw and flat bar, remove any boards left attached to the rails.

2. Knock off the remaining pieces with a hammer and remove the staples with the vice grips.

3. Place the 3 rails on their sides on the sawhorses. Measure and mark three 37" (94cm) pieces and two 15" (38cm) pieces on the first rail. This will give you 3 pieces for the top and 2 end pieces for the sides. On the second rail, measure and mark three 37" (94cm) pieces. This will give you 2 pieces for the top and 1 piece for the front. On the third rail, measure and mark one 37" (94cm) piece for the back and four 18" (46cm) pieces for the legs. Cut the pieces at each mark with the chop saw.

4. Lay the pieces out and arrange to create the look you desire. Sand each piece. Sanding at this point ensures smooth surfaces and edges even on the center pieces.

5. As you trim and cut each piece, return it to the laid-out design. This will help you identify the pieces as you assemble the bench. Starting with the top pieces, trim one end and cut to 36" (91cm). Take the front and back pieces, trim one end and cut to 35" (89cm). Trim and cut each side piece to 14" (36cm). Dry fit your pieces and make any adjustments.

6. To create the frame, take a front and side piece. Predrill and place 2 screws at each corner. Repeat on the next 3 corners, attaching the other side and back pieces.

7. Lay the frame flat and use a hammer to make any adjustments to ensure a level surface. Trim and cut the leg pieces to 16½" (42cm). Inspect your leg pieces and choose the best ones for the front. Decide how you want to position the legs. The wide side of the board can face to the front or to the side. Either position will provide the same stability; it is just a matter of how you want the bench to look.

8. Attach a clamp to a top piece and the frame to position the leg flush with the top.

9. Predrill and screw into place using 2 screws. Repeat on the remaining legs.

10. Dry fit the top pieces again to double check for proper fit, and arrange to achieve the look you desire. Allow a ½" (12mm) overhang on the front and sides. The ends should be flush with the frame on each end. Position a common nail between each top piece to space the boards evenly.

11. Use a nail gun to place 2 small nails into the top of each board to secure the boards in place and to attach to the frame.

12. Predrill and place a screw in the center of each board to secure to the frame. Predrilling will keep the board from spitting and will allow the screw to have a better fit.

13. Sand any rough edges and finish as you like. Place under your favorite shade tree and embrace your royalty!

PROJECTS FOR YOUR HOME

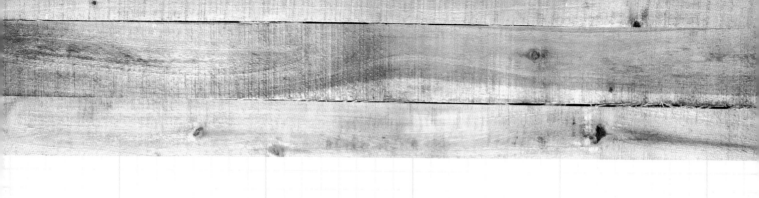

Flower & Candle Crate

What room isn't made even more inviting when you fill it with a beautiful display of fresh flowers and glowing candles?

This is a great project that allows you to bring the beauty of your garden inside or to fill the jars with candles and create a warm environment in any room! This cute crate is a pretty simple project that is fun to make and is very versatile. It is designed to fit three 1-quart mason jars. It can be adjusted in measurements to fit any size jar or glass you desire. Choose the color and markings of the pallet pieces to create the look you want. The wood can be painted, stained, clear coated, or left unfinished depending on the desired look. Make several, so you can spread them around the room for an even prettier effect. They can be used in any season and filled with anything fun and beautiful.

We made a few of these at Thanksgiving and used them down the middle of the table as centerpieces filled with flowers, candles, and gourds. It was both festive and beautiful.

They will brighten up any space and even make a great gift!

BEST SIZE/SHAPE PALLET TO USE

Any size

TOOLS

- Jigsaw
- Tape measure
- Portable table saw
- End nippers
- Portable drill

MATERIALS

- 1 pallet, any size (doesn't really matter because you are cutting pieces to size)
- 1 – 11 ½" x 4" (29 x 10cm) piece
- 1 ¼" (30mm) brads
- 2 – 4 ½" x 4" (11 x 10cm) pieces
- Wood glue
- 4 – 2" x 12 ½" (5 x 32cm) pieces
- 3 – 1-quart (1-liter) mason jars

1. Use a jigsaw to cut 5 boards from the pallet.

2. Trim pieces to size on the table saw.

3. Dry fit your pieces, trimming if necessary to ensure a proper fit. If the end pieces have a slight bow, position the curve to the inside. You can sand the box flat by hand or with a belt sander when the box is finished, if necessary.

4. Use the end nippers to remove the head of a brad and insert it into the drill chuck. Set aside.

5. Begin assembling the crate by building the base. Place a thin line of wood glue down the center of the end piece, allowing a little space on each end to prevent any glue from squeezing to outside surfaces.

6. Align and hold the bottom and side pieces together. Drill 3 holes along the bottom edge with the brad nail bit. Predrilling the holes will prevent the pieces from splitting. There is no need to let the glue dry before drilling.

7. Hammer a brad into each hole, attaching the base to the side piece. Repeat the process on the other end.

8. Dry fit the bottom side rail, checking for correct fit; trim if necessary. Place a thin line of glue along the bottom and side edges. Drill 1 hole on each end to attach and then 3 along the bottom edge. Hammer brads into each hole.

9. Line up the top rail with the top edge of the end piece. Place a small line of glue and drill 2 holes at the end of each piece that line up with the brads on the bottom board. Repeat on the other side.

10. Sand any rough edges. Paint or stain if desired and fill with mason jars.

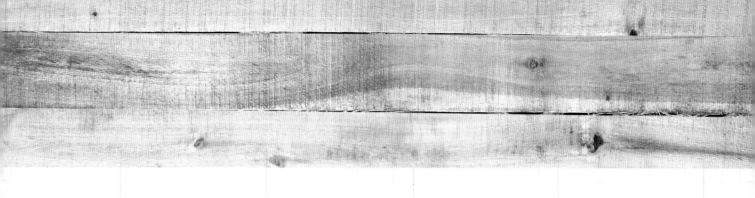

Tiered Plant Stand

Are you looking for a way to add a little design element to your living space that would showcase a seasonal display or small collection? This little tiered plant stand might become your new favorite thing!

This is a fun project to display your favorite decorations, collections, and plants. If you have space on your kitchen counter, you could even fill it with potted herbs.

There is not a lot of space on the shelves, but it adds a lot of character to any room. The top shelf could also be filled with candles for a beautiful ambiance.

It is a project that has a couple of neat structural and woodworking techniques.

It can be painted, stained, clear coated, or left unfinished, whatever will make your display shine all the more!

BEST SIZE/SHAPE PALLET TO USE

42" x 42" (107 x 107cm)

TOOLS

- Jigsaw
- Nail gun
- Chop saw with fence
- Staple gun
- Table saw
- Hammer
- Tape measure

MATERIALS

- 1 pallet, 42" x 42"
- Wood glue
- 5 – 1" (25mm) staples for the staple gun
- 2 – 2 ½" (60mm) nails for the nail gun

1. Use the jigsaw to cut the wide plank board along the inside of the stringer board on both sides. These are your shelf pieces.

2. Cut 3 thinner plank boards the same way, giving you 6 pieces. These are the frame and cap pieces. Set the chop saw to a 50° angle. Cut 4 of the pieces.

3. Set the table saw fence to 2" (5cm).

4. Cut the 4 frame pieces.

5. Lay out your pieces and mark the lower edge of each leg to make it level with the floor.

6. Reset the chop saw to 40° and cut the fifth piece. Flip and cut one more piece, creating two cap pieces for the frame. Dry fit each side of the frame.

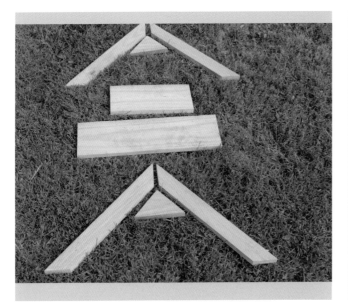

7. Cut the bottom edge of each frame piece on a 40° angle to make it flush with the floor. Reset the chop saw to 90° and trim both ends of one shelf piece to create clean edges. It should be approximately 18" (46cm). Trim one end of the second shelf and cut to 11" (28cm). Lay out your pieces to make sure everything aligns.

8. Place a thin line of glue on the top edge of a frame piece. Hold flush to the other piece and use a nail gun to attach the pieces together on both sides of the tip. Repeat with the second frame.

9. Place a line of glue on the cap piece and attach it to the frame with 4 staples along the bottom edge and 2 closer to the tip. Repeat on the second frame.

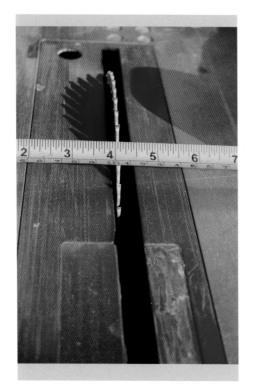

10. Set the fence on the table saw to 4" (10cm) and cut a scrap piece of wood for a spacer. Cut the length in half with the chop saw.

11. Dry fit the bottom shelf with the spacers in place and use a clamp to hold in place.

12. Attach with 2 nails on each frame side. Repeat on other side.

13. Place spacer on top of bottom shelf and align the top shelf. Clamp and nail as before.

14. Paint or stain as desired.

Headboard

Ahhhh . . . there is nothing more restful than a beautiful, cozy bedroom! And a beautiful, custom-made headboard will make your room even more amazing. Building your own headboard isn't necessary, but it can add a lot character to your space. Bringing a bit of the outdoors in can also add a layer of texture and design.

This is a great project because you really can design any pattern you want! The plank boards can be hung vertically, horizontally, or arranged in a specific design. They can be all the same size and shape or a variety, sanded and painted or left natural—the possibilities are endless!

You just need to choose the size of frame you need and then place support pieces where needed. We purchased 2" x 4" (50 x 100cm) pieces to create the frame just to provide a sturdy, uniform base, but you can use pallet stringer boards if you have the length needed.

Headboards are designed to be 3" (8cm) wider than the mattress's length. Standard sizes are 42" (107cm) for a twin; 61" (155cm) for a full/double; 63" (160cm) for a queen and 79" (200cm) for a king. You can choose the height you want for your particular style and space. We created a king-size headboard that is 4' (122cm) tall for this example.

We love the look of pallet boards that vary in stages of both color and texture. We chose to incorporate several boards with stamps, markings, and nail holes just to add to its unique design.

This is where it will come in handy to have some extra boards that you have set aside from other projects to use. If you don't, no worries, you can still achieve the look you want by gathering pallets that have the specific color and character you want. It might also be fun to do this project with a friend and share the wood from several pallets!

We chose to attach the boards with finishing nails so that the boards would be the focus, but you could also choose to use flat head nails or any other nail to add the look you want.

The main thing is to dry fit your design on your frame before you start building, to ensure proper support for all the boards. You want to be certain that they can all be attached to some part of the frame.

The instructions below will help you construct the frame. Adjust the height and width of the measurements for the size you want. Add or reduce the number of support beams to fit your design.

Make sure to measure to ensure your finished piece can fit in the doors and stairways that you will need to take it through before assembling!

So get creative, come up with an awesome design, and begin laying it out. You're not locked in until you start adding the nails!

BEST SIZE/SHAPE PALLET TO USE

2 or 3 of any size, depending on the design and material you want

TOOLS

- Jigsaw or Sawzall
- Tape measure
- Chop saw with fence
- Nail gun
- Table saw
- Portable drill

MATERIALS

- 2 or 3 pallets, any size or length (determined by the pattern and color design you want)
- 2 ½" (60mm) nails for the nail gun
- 3" (75mm) screws

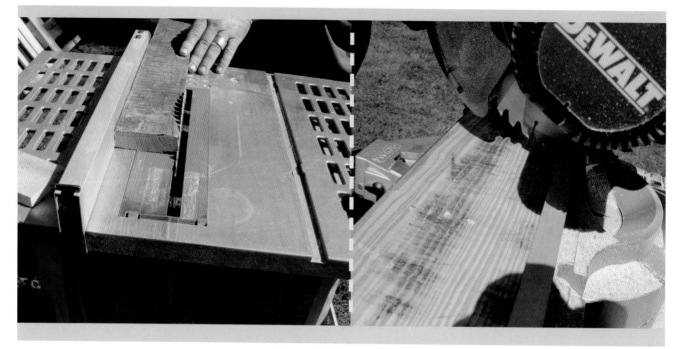

1. Determine the size of your frame and the design you want for the headboard. Remove the plank boards from the pallets using the techniques described in other projects for the look and character you want. Remove the nails, and trim and cut the pieces to size with the table and chop saws. Set aside.

2. Begin to build the frame by attaching the fence to the chop saw. Set the fence stop to the length you need for the top and bottom pieces. Trim one end for a clean edge, then flip and cut two 2" x 4"'s (50 x 100cm). Reset the stop and trim, then cut four pieces for the support beams.

3. Lay the pieces out on a flat, stable surface. Dry fit the frame and divide the width by 3 to determine the placement of the 2 middle support pieces.

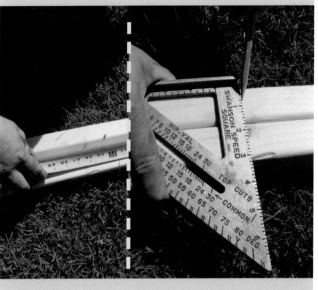

4. Hold the top and bottom frame pieces together on their sides and mark with a pencil.

5. Lay the center support pieces flat and mark the center.

6. Hold the corner pieces together and attach with 2 nails for stability (they will be reinforced with screws later in the process). Repeat with the second top corner.

7. Line up the center support pieces with the top and bottom marks. Place an extra piece of a 2" x 4" (50 x 100cm) under the board as support to make it flush with the front of the top frame, then nail in place. Repeat with the second support, then attach the bottom frame.

8. Predrill and place 2 screws in each joint with a portable drill.

9. Dry fit the pieces for the headboard, making any adjustments. Nail the pieces in place with a nail gun.

10. Sand any rough edges and finish as desired. Sweet dreams!

Wall-Mounted Coat Rack

No matter what season it is, you'll find so many reasons to add this awesome coat rack to your living space! It will help you stay organized on a daily basis with the things we tend to misplace the most. Whether you hang it in your entranceway, your mudroom, or the kitchen, it will be the best place to hang your coat, your hat, your umbrella, your pet's leash, your keys, your purse, and even the book bags!

It has a sturdy design and will add a lot of character to wherever you choose to use it. It's made with the full width of the pallet but can also be made with half, if you don't have the space. We show you how to make it with a solid top, but you can cut a 1 ½' (46cm) piece from the top board, add a hinge and a bottom piece above the hooks, and you will have additional storage as well! A great place for gloves, scarfs, and the bills you want to hide away.

So you can see that for a simple project, it will come in handy in so many ways!

BEST SIZE/SHAPE PALLET TO USE

48" x 40" (122 x 102cm) with a wider plank board on each end and forklift cutouts

TOOLS

- Jigsaw
- Small clamp
- Hammer
- Tape measure
- Sawhorses

MATERIALS

- 1 pallet, 48" x 40", with forklift cutouts
- #4 – 1 ¼" (30mm) common nails
- 80 grit sandpaper
- Hanging hooks
- Paint or stain (optional)

1. Lay the pallet down on the sawhorses or a steady surface with the forklift cutouts facing up.

2. Measure and mark the center of the smallest cut closest to the bottom board. Every forklift cut is different, so we use the smallest one to create balance.

3. Measure and mark the same length on the center stringer board and the other end. Starting with the center board, use the jigsaw to cut each mark.

4. Remove the wide board from the top of the pallet with a flat bar from the end to prevent splitting. Remove the nails. This will become the top ledge.

5. Use the small clamp to stand the rack up with the narrowest part at the bottom. Dry fit the top piece and then secure with a nail at each end and at the center.

6. Place a second nail at each location to secure to the frame.

7. Sand any rough edges. At this point you can paint or stain to your liking, or leave the boards natural for a more rustic look. Lay the coat rack down on a steady surface, measure the lower board, and mark the center for the hook placement.

8. Lay out the hooks you are using along the center mark. Check for alignment, then predrill (if oak) and attach the hooks.

9. Mount directly to the wall, making sure to attach it to a stud or use a mounting anchor. You're ready to go!

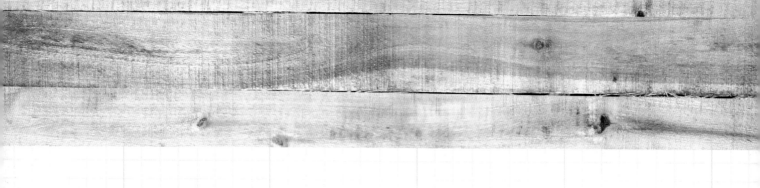

Spice Rack

So many spices, so little time! No matter how many spices you may have in your spice rack, it's always fun to try something new. New flavors, new recipes, new adventures in food!

Whether you only have salt, pepper, and olive oil on your shelves, or you have a full array of spices, it is great to keep them displayed and handy. This little spice rack will look fantastic in your kitchen and might even inspire you to try something beyond your old standards. There are three shelves that give you just enough room to explore. It is sturdy and has a "nailer" piece that will help you secure it to the wall.

If you need more space, you can adjust the width or make two and hang them side by side. It can be painted or stained to match your kitchen décor.

So, take an inventory of your spice collection and be inspired to add new amazing cooking adventures!

BEST SIZE/SHAPE PALLET TO USE

42" x 42" (107 x 107cm)

TOOLS

- Jigsaw
- Brad gun
- Chop saw
- Quick grip clamp
- Tape measure
- 80 grit sandpaper

MATERIALS

- 1 pallet, 42" x 42"
- 1 ½" (40mm) brads
- Wood glue

2. Trim one end and then cut two 18" (46cm) pieces for the sides and three 12½" (32cm) pieces for the shelves with the chop saw.

1. Cut 9 plank boards similar in width along the inner edge of the center and outer stringer board.

3. Trim and cut two 12½" (32cm) pieces with the chop saw for the "nailer" pieces. These will be used to secure the spice rack to the wall.

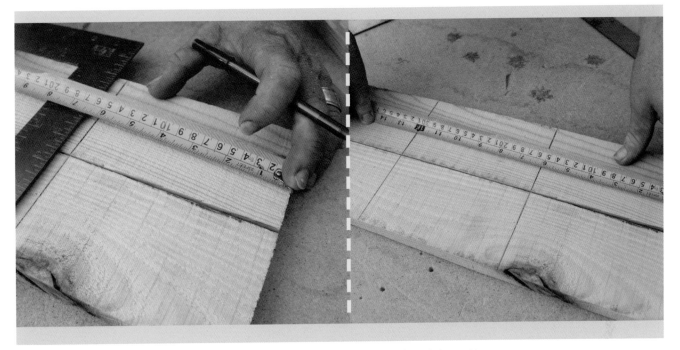

4. Measure and mark the side pieces at 6" (15cm) and 12" (30cm) from the bottom edge.

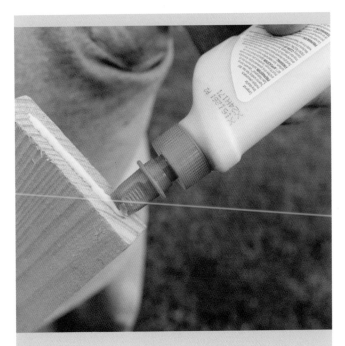

5. Place a thin line of glue on the bottom shelf piece and hold it flush with a side piece.

6. Place 3 brads along the bottom edge to attach.

7. Repeat with the second and third shelves, lining them up with the 6" (15cm) and 12" (30cm) marks.

8. Lay the side piece on its back and place a thin line of glue on each shelf end.

9. Place the second side piece flush with the bottom shelf and place 3 brads to attach each shelf to the side.

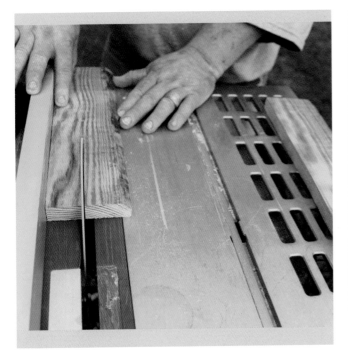

10. Cut 5 pieces to 1½" (40mm) width with the table saw. These are the front edge and nailer pieces.

11. Trim and cut 3 pieces to 14" (36cm). These are the front edge pieces.

12. Place a thin line of glue along the side and bottom edges of the bottom shelf.

13. Hold the front piece in place and place 2 brads in each end and 3 brads along the front edge to secure to the frame. Repeat with the next two shelves.

14. Place a thin line of glue along the sides and edge of the first nailer piece.

15. Hold flush to the back edge of the frame and under the middle shelf. Use a clamp to hold it in place. Repeat on the upper shelf.

16. Use the brad gun to secure the piece to the frame with 2 brads on each side placed closely together.

17. Place an additional brad in the middle of the shelf.

18. Sand and finish as you like.

Tabletop Herb Box

This little herb box was inspired by Steve's grandmother who always had herbs growing on her kitchen counter. She was a great cook and would love to add "just a bit of this" and "a bit of that." She grew up in the mountains where herbs were plentiful, and she loved to use them to cook and make tea, as well as a few concoctions to make you better! The smells from her kitchen are some of his favorite childhood memories.

This box will hold about three herbs plants, so you can make a few if you need more room. It is a simple, sturdy box that could actually be used for all sorts of things. But our favorite use will always be for herbs and good memories!

Leave natural or finish the outside to create the look you desire.

BEST SIZE/SHAPE PALLET TO USE

Any with plank boards that measure at least 5" (13cm) in width

TOOLS

- Jigsaw
- Tape measure
- Portable drill
- Speed square or combination square
- Table saw with fence
- End nippers
- Hammer

MATERIALS

- 1 pallet, any size, with wide boards
- Wood glue
- 1 ¼" (30mm) brads
- 80 grit sandpaper

1. Cut 6 plank boards along the inner edge of the center and outer stringer boards to remove from the pallet. Set the fence on the table saw to 5⅛" (130mm). Trim each piece on one side to create a clean edge.

2. Set the fence to 5" (127mm). Flip each piece over and trim the other side.

3. Use the cross-cut gauge to cut a clean end on each board.

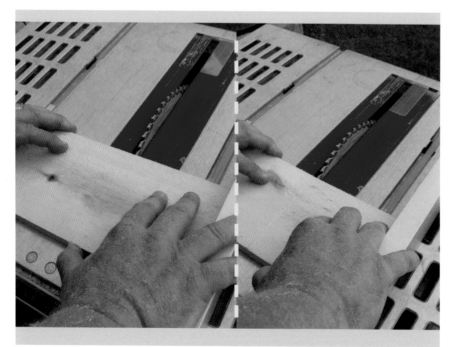

4. Select which boards you want for the ends, side, and base of the box. If the boards have a little bow to them, place the curve to the inside. The finished box can be sanded flat. Measure, mark, and cut two 5" (127mm) pieces for the ends.

5. Measure, mark, and cut two 16" (40cm) pieces for the sides.

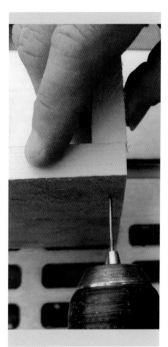

6. Cut the head off of a brad with the end nippers and insert into the drill chuck. Set aside. Dry fit a side piece and end piece.

7. Starting ¼" (6mm) from the edge, place a thin line of glue on the bottom of one end piece.

8. Line up with the base and predrill a hole that is ½" (12mm) from each end.

9. Hammer a brad into each hole to attach.

10. Repeat with 2 more brads in between.

11. Repeat on the other 3 corners. Predrilling prevents the pieces from splitting and creates a more finished look.

12. Place one end of the base piece in the box. Measure, mark, and cut to length.

13. Place the bottom into the box and hammer flush.

14. Predrill and nail 5 brads along the bottom edge. Repeat on the other side. There is no need for glue, as the brads will hold the base in place. Predrill and nail 3 brads along the bottom edge of each end.

15. Sand and finish as you like.

Serving Tray

Whether you are enjoying a cup of hot tea on a quiet afternoon, serving your favorite someone breakfast in bed, or running things out to the grill, this beautiful serving tray will help you do it in style! It is nice and sturdy and will come in handy in so many ways.

The details will remind you that it is indeed a pallet project, but its simple elegance will be the thing you notice the most. We used the forklift cutouts to form the handles because they are easy to hold onto and fit the frame perfectly!

Choose a pallet with wide boards that have a grain pattern or detail that you will love featuring as the surface of the tray. You can give it a layer of clear coat, paint, or stain or just leave it as is. A cut piece of glass can be added, too, for extra protection.

This is a project that you'll love to make and have around, but we have to say that it makes a great housewarming or wedding gift!

TOOLS

- Sawzall
- Hammer
- Sawhorses or a working surface
- Tape measure
- Flat bar
- Framing square
- Jigsaw
- Chop saw
- Table saw
- Orbital sander
- Staple gun
- Nail gun

MATERIALS

- 1 pallet, 40" x 48"
- 50 grit sandpaper
- 2" (50mm) finish nails for the nail gun

BEST SIZE/SHAPE PALLET TO USE

40" x 48" (102 x 122 cm)

1. Measure and mark 3½" (90mm) on both sides of the forklift cutout.

2. Draw a line on the stringer board up to the top edge just past the left measurement that is between 2 plank boards. You will cut along this line to separate the piece used for the tray away from the pallet. Use the Sawzall to cut the center and end stringer boards away from the rest of the pallet.

3. Use a framing square to draw a straight line along the outside edge of the center stringer board up to the end.

4. Use a jigsaw to cut the plank boards on the top; flip the pallet over and cut the bottom boards.

5. Remove the plank boards from the stringer boards with a flat bar and hammer. Start with the center boards, keeping the end boards in place for stability, then remove the end boards.

6. Remove 3 long plank boards from the extra part of the pallet and 3 boards from the smaller piece.

7. Hammer the nails back through the boards and remove with the claw end of the hammer.

8. Cut along the 3½" (90mm) line on the each handle piece with the chop saw.

9. Trim and cut the plank boards to 21" (53cm). These boards are the side and base pieces of the tray.

10. Measure the length of the handle pieces and cut one of the plank boards to match.

11. Cut a clean edge with the table saw and then set the fence to 1½" (40mm). Cut again to end up with 2 "feet" for under the tray.

12. Lay the pieces out and arrange them in the order you want for the tray surface.

13. Sand the pieces with the orbital sander to create a smooth surface.

14. Dry fit the tray base and place the "foot" piece alongside to determine the amount that needs to be trimmed, and mark with a pencil. Trim with the table saw. You can also center the piece and trim both end pieces if you prefer.

15. Lay a framing square along the side edge to hold the pieces flush.

16. Attach the feet to each end with a staple gun (2 staples per board).

17. Sand the handle pieces with the orbital sander. Attach the feet to the base and handle with the nail gun (2 nails per end).

18. Measure and mark 1½" (40mm) beyond the handle cutout to establish the tray height.

19. Measure and mark the side piece to match.

20. Adjust the table saw fence and cut the handle side to height.

21. Measure and mark the distance from the tray bottom edge to the tray height.

22. Adjust the table saw fence and cut the tray side pieces.

23. Attach the sides to the tray with the nail gun (2 nails on each end).

24. Sand any rough edges.

25. Finish the tray any way you like and you are ready to serve!

Tea Light/Votive Holder

A room filled with candlelight is a beautiful thing! It can help you relax at the end of the day and is a great way to create cozy ambiance to spend time with dear friends laughing and chatting the hours away.

This is a really simple project that packs a lot of punch! All you need is a drill bit and a couple of candles, and you can add a lot of charm to your living space. The candles can be grouped together or spread around the room to create the warm atmosphere you want.

The holders are made with the solid wood blocks from the bottom side of a pallet so they are nice and sturdy. We love making some that rest on their side and others that stand on their end for a variety of looks.

You can choose the markings and the amount of weathering on the blocks and decorate them as you like. Paint, stain, or leave them natural for the effect you want. We love utilizing the amazing art skills of our friend and local Baltimore artist Shawn Theron of *SOGH.org* to make some of our pieces true works of art.

It is a great way to use another part of the pallet and complete a project in a matter of minutes!

BEST SIZE/SHAPE PALLET TO USE

The feet blocks from a longer pallet
    Make sure the blocks are solid wood and not compressed board.

TOOLS

- Portable drill
- 1 ½" (40mm) drill bit for a tea light
- 2" (50mm) drill bit for a votive holder

MATERIALS

- Block feet from 31" x 144" pallets
- Tea light or glass votive holder

1. Measure the bottom of the tea light or votive holder to make sure you have the drill bit size you need. Mark the placement of the candles. Sink the drill bit into the block, level with three-quarters the height of the drill bit.

Footstool

This footstool was inspired by Steve's grandfather. He always had a footstool around to help him change out his shoes at the end of a long day and then put his feet up to rest.

This sturdy little stool also works great as a step stool for yourself or your little loves.

It's light and portable, which makes it great to use anywhere indoors, out on your front porch, or out by a fire pit, wherever you need it. You could even keep it in your car trunk for those emergency situations. Its straightforward structure and design makes it easy to make so you can create several to have around your house!

It makes a great gift as well. One of my favorite childhood Christmas gifts was a little stool made by my uncle with my name on it and a picture of Winnie-the-Pooh drawn by my aunt.

However you choose to use it, it is a project that is fun to make and will come in handy in all sorts of ways!

BEST SIZE/SHAPE PALLET TO USE

42" x 55" (107 x 140cm) with wide plank boards – this can be done with a pallet with narrower boards, you would then glue and staple two boards together for the legs.

TOOLS

- Jigsaw
- Flat bar
- Chop saw with fence
- Hammer
- Table saw
- Sawhorses
- Tape measure
- Brad gun

MATERIALS

- 1 pallet, 42" x 55", with at least 1 wide board
- 1 ¼" (30mm) brads
- 80 grit sandpaper
- Wood glue

1. Remove 2 plank boards from the pallet using a hammer and flat bar, being careful not to split the boards.

2. Place the boards on a stable surface, and hammer the nails back through and remove with the claw end of the hammer.

3. Use a jigsaw to cut another plank board along the inner edge of the outside and center stringer boards. This will become the leg pieces.

4. Set up a fence on the chop saw. Set a stop at 7¼" (19cm) on the chop saw. Trim and cut the third plank board, creating two identical pieces.

5. Because of the variation in pallet plank boards, the actual measurements for the top and frame may be slightly different than what we list. The top surface should be approximately 17" (43cm) long, 9½" (24cm) wide, and 8" (20cm) tall. Starting with the widest plank board, cut the first piece to 3¼" (83mm) width on the table saw. Repeat with the second board. Reset the fence, flip the boards over, and trim the other edge of the cut pieces to 3⅛" (79mm). This will give you a clean edge on both sides. You will have 2 boards that measure 3⅛" (79mm) for the top surface and 2 that are a little narrower that will create the frame.

6. Trim one end to create a clean, straight edge. Then flip the board over and cut the top pieces to 17" (43cm) with the chop saw. Place the cut edge of the frame pieces along the fence of the table saw and cut to 2¼" (57mm). Trim and cut two 15" (38cm) pieces and four 6" (15cm) pieces (or the width of the legs) on the chop saw.

7. Center a 4" (10cm) lid halfway up the edge of the first leg and trace around with a pencil to create the cutout. Repeat on the second leg.

8. Nail the two legs together with 2 brads toward the top edge. This will keep the two pieces together while you make the cut, which will ensure two identical cutouts.

9. Cut along the radius with a jigsaw. Pull the boards apart and remove the nails.

10. Begin building the frame by placing a thin line of glue on the inside edge of the first end piece. You do not need to wait for the glue to dry.

11. Hold flush to a side piece and place 2 brads in each corner to secure. Repeat on the other corners.

12. Place a leg piece inside one end of the frame and then a 6" (15cm) piece on top. Attach all 3 pieces together with 2 brads on each end and 1 in the center. Repeat on the other end.

13. Dry fit and make any adjustment cuts, then sand any rough edges.

14. If you are painting the footstool, do that now to coat the inside edges of the top boards. Let dry. We painted the base, frame, bottom, and side edges of the top boards with a solid stroke of paint and then used a light stroke to gently cover the surface, leaving it with a whitewash effect. Lay the center board in place and put 3 brads in each end to secure it to the base. Use brads placed between the boards as spacers and repeat with the other two boards. Put 3 brads along the length of the outer boards to attach to the frame.

15. Stand the stool up and put weight on it to check for stability. Add additional brads if needed and make any adjustments to the legs to ensure stability. You're now ready to sit back, put your feet up, and relax!

Wall-Mounted Bookshelf

This is a great project to use in any room!

It will add a lot of character and function at the same time. It's a decorative way to display and store books in your bedroom, kitchen, or den. The hooks make it easy to hang a robe, kitchen apron, or to store your keys. Get creative with the hooks and add a fun feature that fits your room!

We love using the pallets that are narrow with a center stringer board. This makes the bookshelf a little smaller but works great in a child's room or kitchen.

Add extra boards to the front and back or leave open spaces, depending on the look you want.

It can be pretty heavy once you start filling it with your favorite books, so make sure you mount it well. Now you're ready for that cup of tea!

TOOLS	MATERIALS
• Jigsaw • Table saw • Tape measure • Hammer	• 1 pallet, 48" x 40", with forklift cutouts • #4 – 1 ¼" (30mm) common nails • Paint, stain, or clear coat (optional) • 80 grit sandpaper • Hanging hooks

BEST SIZE/SHAPE PALLET TO USE

48" x 40" (122 x 102cm)

1. Measure and mark the center of the forklift cutout. Measure and mark all 3 stringer boards.

2. Measure and mark the center of the side stringer board. Measure and mark all 3 stringer boards.

3. Use a table saw and jigsaw to cut the stringer boards along the markings.

4. Stand the shelf up and decide if you want to add more boards for the look you want. Remove the additional boards from the pallet, including 1 for the base of the bookshelf. Trim to fit with a table saw and hammer in place on each end and center. We are adding 1 to the front and 2 to the back for this shelf.

5. Measure the width and the length of each base opening.

6. Cut and trim the board for the bases. Dry fit, make any adjustments, and hammer into place.

7. Secure each base in place by placing 3 nails along the base line of each section. Flip the pallet over and repeat on the back.

9. Mount to the wall, lining up with a stud or using anchors.

8. Sand all surfaces and rough edges. Paint, stain, apply clear coat, or leave unfinished for your desired look. Place the hooks in the location you want. Predrill and screw into the board to secure.

Menu & Welcome Sign

There is nothing more enjoyable than having family and friends over for a cozy meal!

These cute signs will welcome your guests before you even answer the door and then entice them with the meal plan before they take their first bite!

They are portable and easy to update, so you can use them to direct your guests on where to park, how to find the pool party in the backyard, or to announce the hours of the neighborhood block party.

They are made in a pair with a long, narrow pallet that we make even narrower with a few adjustments and then cut in half for the set. You can choose to make one longer and one shorter if you have a specific space in mind, but we like the matching ones that can be used together or on their own.

The blackboard paint is a fun feature that allows you to change the message anytime you want! The signs are sturdy and stand on their own or can gently lean back in a corner for added effect. You can use regular paint and write or design a permanent message as well.

They also make a great gift that could display marriage or birth information, encouraging words, etc. The possibilities are endless!

This is a pretty simple project that we think you will have fun making and will come up with even more ideas for their use. Get your kids involved and help them hone their woodworking and painting skills!

BEST SIZE/SHAPE PALLET TO USE

Because you are going to create the width you want the main feature to look for in a pallet is the size and number of boards. You will want them to have enough space to write a message: 8"x 48" (46 x 122cm) with 8 boards

TOOLS	MATERIALS	
• Jigsaw	• 1 pallet, 48" x 72"	• Paint primer
• Tape measure	• 1 ½" (40mm) common nails	• Chalkboard paint
• Hammer	• Clamps	• Small paint roller
	• 80 grit sandpaper	

1. Lay the pallet down on a level, secure surface. Decide how wide you want your message boards to be. The rail will be attached to the underside, so make sure the length you choose is the full surface space you want. Measure and mark the plank boards. Cut to length with a jigsaw. (If you have a narrow pallet and you are happy with it as it is, you won't need to cut and reattach a side stringer board).

2. Use the jigsaw to cut along the inside rail of each plank board to remove the stringer board.

3. Flip the pallet over and repeat on the other side. This will allow you to create the width you want by attaching a new side.

4. Use the hammer to knock off the extra pieces of wood around the nails.

5. Use the claw end of the hammer to remove each nail.

6. If the nail head breaks off in the process, use vice grips or channel locks to remove the rest of the nail.

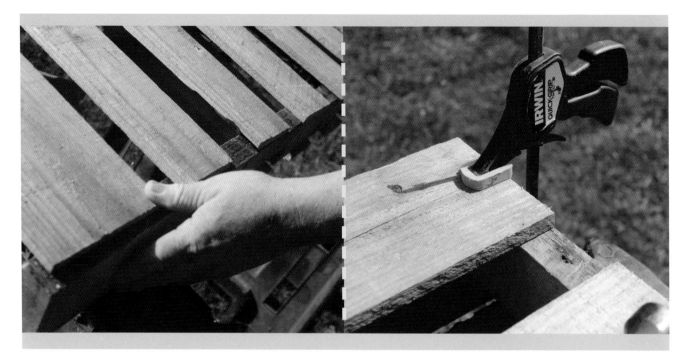

7. Lay the pallet on sawhorses or a secure surface. Line up the new stringer board and use clamps to hold the pieces together.

8. Hammer the new nails in each end of the boards, lining them up to match the nails at the other end. They do not need to match in color since you will be painting over them.

9. Mark the center distance between the fourth and fifth boards on both sides. This is to create two signs of the same size. If you want to change the size, just mark and cut to the size you want.

10. Use a jigsaw to cut the signs apart.

11. Sand the surfaces smooth and any rough edges.

12. Place the signs side by side and inspect for any loose boards or anything that needs adjusting.

13. Paint with primer and chalkboard paint according to manufacturer's directions.

14. Let dry and get your party started!

Tall Side Table

We can all use a little more serving space when we have people over! This tall side table fits the bill. It is portable and sturdy and is just the right height for serving.

It is perfect for hors d'oeuvres and snacks or can be used as an extra staging area for plates, glasses, and utensils. It can be moved wherever you need it for added convenience. The lower shelf is great to keep extra supplies on hand.

Using two pallets to create the table will allow you to pick the plank boards with the character you want. There is quite a bit of detail in making this table, but we think you will find it is worth the effort! It may also show you some new techniques and skills.

So, take your time and make it right, and then serve yourself a snack to celebrate!

TOOLS

- Jigsaw
- Portable drill with ³⁄₁₆" (5mm) bit
- Table saw
- Brad gun
- Chop saw with fence
- Flat bar
- Handsaw
- Chisel
- Tape measure

MATERIALS

- 2 pallets, 42" x 42"
- Wood glue
- 1 ⅝" (41mm) screws
- 1 ¼" (30mm) brads for the brad gun

BEST SIZE/SHAPE PALLET TO USE

2 – 42" x 42" (107 x 107cm) with solid stringer boards (no forklift cutouts)

1. Cut 5 of the wider plank boards along the outer stringer boards with a jigsaw and remove from the center, going with the grain, with a flat bar. Hammer the nails back through and remove. Set aside. These pieces will be used for the tabletop and lower shelf.

2. Cut 4 pieces from the narrower boards along the outer and center stringer boards with a jigsaw. Cut 4 narrower boards along the outer stringer boards and remove from the center with a flat bar as you did with the wide boards, or pull the board up and remove. These pieces will become the upper and lower frame/apron.

3. Lay the 8 frame pieces on their sides and choose the narrowest board.

4. Set the fence of the table saw to 3¼" (83mm) and trim all the pieces on one side to create a clean edge.

5. Reset the fence to 3" (76mm), flip the boards over, and trim the other sides.

7. Reset the fence to 16" (40cm) and repeat the process on the 4 shorter boards. Begin building the upper apron by taking one of the 16" (40cm) pieces, placing a thin line of glue on one end, and holding it flush to the inside of a 29" (74cm) piece to create an L. Attach the boards with

6. Take the 4 longer pieces and trim one end; then cut to 29" (74cm) on the chop saw. Set the fence stop to 29" (74cm) and repeat on the next 3 pieces.

3 brads. Place the second 16" (40cm) piece on the inside edge of the other end and secure with the glue and brads. Place glue on the two shorter piece edges and attach the next 29" (74cm) piece with 3 brads on each corner. Predrill a hole in each corner and fill with a screw for added stability. Predrilling will prevent the wood from splitting. Repeat for the second apron.

8. Remove the nails and any wood pieces from the 3 stringer boards from each pallet. You will use 4 of these pieces for the table legs. The other 2 can be used for another project. Trim your first piece on one end and cut to 34" (86cm) on the chop saw. Set the fence stop and repeat on the next 3 legs. Choose the pieces you want for the front legs and decide whether you want the wide part of the board facing to the front or to the side. Hold the first leg flush with the top edge of the first apron. Predrill and place 2 screws in each leg to attach it to the frame. Repeat with the next 3 legs.

9. Cut 2 pieces of scrap wood to 14" (36cm) with the chop saw to use as spacers. Place the spacers between the two aprons and attach the legs to the second frame.

10. Dry fit your top pieces and arrange the pattern you want. Place any curving of the plank board down toward the frame. The top surface should measure 18" (46cm) in depth. Trim and cut to 30" (76cm) with the chop saw. Dry fit again and position the front board with a 1" (25mm) overhang on the front and ½" (12mm) on the side. Place 2 brads on the side and 1 along the front edge to hold the board in place.

11. Use 2 common nails as spacers and place 2 brads on each end of each board until you get to the last board.

12. Measure the distance from the spacer nail to the back edge of the apron to determine the width of the last board.

13. Adjust the fence and cut to fit on the table saw. Attach with the brads.

14. Predrill and place 1 screw in the middle of each board along the end to attach to the frame.

15. To create the notches in the shelf board, first line up and mark the depth on the inside leg.

16. Place the board on the outside of the frame and mark.

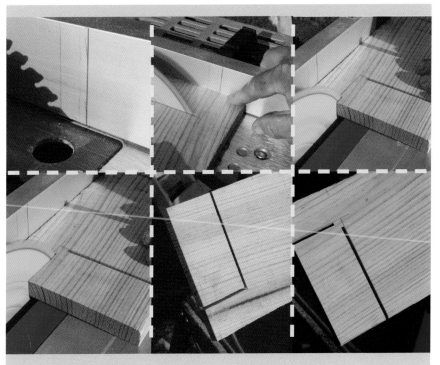

17. Repeat with the other end and second outside piece.

18. Adjust the fence on the table saw to line up with the first line. Cut until the line drawn aligns with the line on the saw. Turn the board and cut to the other line.

19. Cut the rest of the corner with a handsaw and use a chisel to make a clean corner. Repeat on all 4 corners.

20. Dry fit your board and make any adjustments.

21. Hold one of the center boards flush with the right side edge and mark the board underneath along the frame edge.

22. Cut on the table saw.

23. Measure the distance between the outside board and the center board. Cut the last piece to fit.

24. Dry fit the pieces.

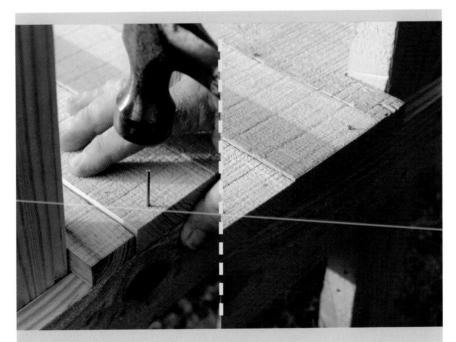

25. Nail the center boards to the frame with 2 nails on each end.

Wall-Mounted Wine Rack

There are so many wonderful things in life to celebrate, and a lot of times that means that you'll be hosting a crowd! This beautiful wine rack will help you stay organized as you let the celebration flow.

This is a great project to make for yourself or to give as a gift! Its overall appearance can make it the focal point of any living space. Its straightforward design not only gives you a beautiful way to store your wine and glasses but also keeps them at the ready for unexpected guests or a quiet night in front of a warm fireplace.

The instructions below are for a full-length rack that will hold up to 12 bottles and 8 glasses, but it can also be made as a half rack, holding up to 6 bottles and 4 glasses if you have a smaller space. You can fill it with your favorite wines or other beverages that fit the shelf. We have even included our favorite olive oils and vinegars for a mix of drinks and appetizers! It works great with bottled waters as well for a refreshment station.

The back can be left with open areas or filled in with additional plank boards—it is totally up to you and your design ideas. Sometimes the pallet you are working with will lead the way with the best look. It is an impressive piece that can be left rustic or can be painted or stained. It can be hung inside or out for indoor or outdoor entertaining. Or maybe one for each place!

This is a fun project to do with great results. They make great wedding and housewarming gifts as well!

BEST SIZE/SHAPE PALLET TO USE

48" x 40" (122 x 102cm) with forklift cutouts

Make sure to select a pallet with fork lift cut outs on the lower stringer boards as you will use that part of the pallet for your project. Also choose one with a nice strong board to use as the wine glass rack. You can even use a board from a separate pallet if needed. Keep these features in mind when selecting your project piece.

TOOLS

- Jigsaw
- Tape measure
- Portable drill with ³⁄₁₆" (5mm) bit and ½" (12mm) bit
- Hammer
- Sawhorses

MATERIALS

- 1 pallet, 48" x 40", with forklift cutouts
- 1 ½" (40mm) brads
- #4 – 1 ½" (40mm) common nails
- 2 ½" (60mm) screws
- 80 grit sandpaper

1. Lay the pallet down on the sawhorses or a steady surface with the forklift cutouts facing up. Measure and mark the center of the smallest cutout closest to the bottom board. There will be one on both the left and right sides of the pallet. Choose the smaller one. Using the smaller one as the guide for your measurements will give your wine rack a balanced look.

2. Measure and mark the length from the bottom board to the center mark.

3. Measure and mark the same length on the center stringer board and the other end board. Cut at each mark using a jigsaw.

4. Remove 3 additional boards with a flat bar and hammer, being careful not to split the boards.

5. If necessary, use a block of wood to separate the board from the stringer boards. Remove the nails.

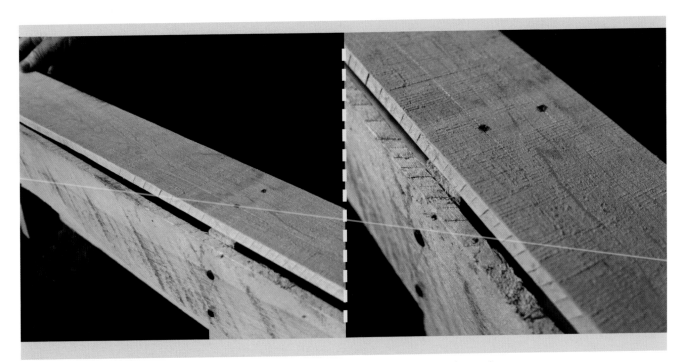

6. Decide which board is the best for the rack base, the stemware rack, and an additional board for the front. Sand the rack base. Dry fit the base piece, placing it flush with the front of the center stringer.

7. Hammer a brad into the center of each stringer board to hold the base in place.

8. Cut three 1½" (40mm) pieces from a stringer board to create "feet" for the stemware rack. These will provide additional support and spacing, and will make the pieces easier to assemble. Predrill the first "foot" with the ³⁄₁₆" (5mm) bit. This prevents the wood from splitting. Place a screw in each foot to attach them to the base. Repeat on the center and end stringer boards.

9. Dry fit the stemware rack piece, and mark the inside edge of the center and end stringer boards.

The instructions below are based on a standard 11.5-oz. white wine glass. It you want it to hold wider red wine glasses or you have a particular stem size, lay the glasses out and make the cut marks on the board.

10. Starting from the outside inner edge, measure and mark 3¼" (83mm) then 3½" (89mm) four times, moving toward the center to create the proper spacing for the stemware. Repeat on the other end, again working toward the center.

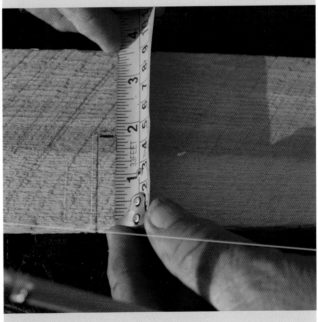

11. Measure and mark the center of the board, and draw your cut lines from each edge.

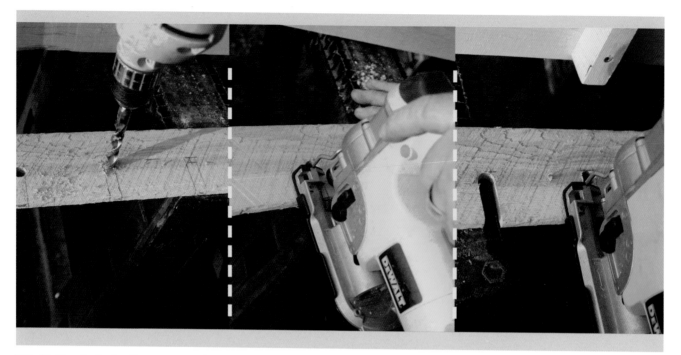

12. Drill a hole in the center of the board and then cut from the edge with a jigsaw to create the stem channel. Slide your stemware into each slot to make sure the width and the spacing of the channel is what you want. Make any adjustment cuts.

13. Attach the stem rack to each foot with 2 nails.

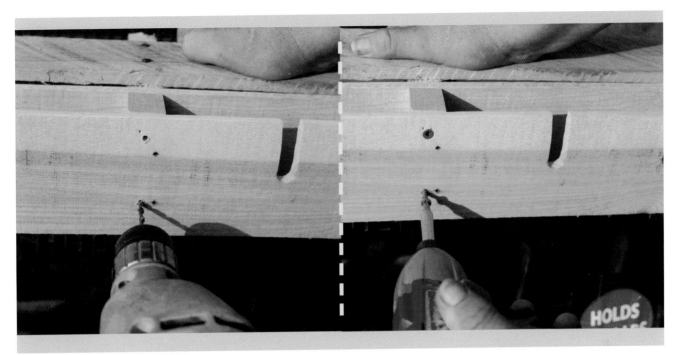

14. Predrill and then replace with 2½" (60mm) screws on either side of the center screw that attaches the foot to the base.

15. Secure any loose front boards with the nails of your choice and decide if any additional boards are needed on the back. Also decide how you are going to hang the rack, and fill in or leave space for the mounting parts. This is a heavy project when filled with full wine bottles and stemware, so make sure to secure it well wherever it is hung. Be sure to attach it to a stud in the wall for best results. You are now ready to sand, finish, and enjoy!

Wall Sconces

This is a fun, simple project that can be used in a variety of ways! The sconces are designed to hang on a wall but could also be placed on a dresser, shelf, entryway table, or mantle. You can hang them in a pair, on their own, or even in a group. They will add both beauty and function to your space however you choose to use them.

You can use any color of pallet and can paint or stain to your desired look. We used an oxidized pallet to make the one pictured and used a little leather polish to cover the freshly cut edges. We also cut the boards in a way that would display as much of the natural patina as we could. They look great with candles, small plants, and, of course, fresh flowers!

TOOLS

- Jigsaw
- Brad gun
- Chop saw

MATERIALS

- 1 pallet, any size, with wide boards
- Wood glue
- 1 ¼" (30mm) brads for the brad gun

BEST SIZE/SHAPE PALLET TO USE

Any with 3"–5" (76 x 127mm) wide plank boards

1. Use a jigsaw to cut three 17" (43cm) pieces from the pallet. Use the chop saw to trim a clean edge and then cut two 12" (30cm) pieces. This will give you a clean edge on each end.

2. Place the chop saw at a 45° angle. Make the first cut.

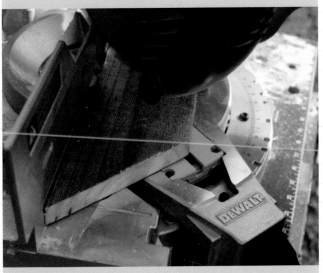

3. Flip the board over and make a second 45° cut.

4. Flip the board over again and place the first cut on top of the second piece to cut to size.

The next cuts are made to ensure the original finish is exposed on the final project. If you are using wood that doesn't need to have a certain edge exposed, you can jump over the additional cut. You can also choose the size of your accent angle at this point. You can leave them a little larger or make them the smaller size shown in the pictures. It is up to you. Dry fit the pieces and see what you prefer.

5. Place desired finishes to the inside and stack one on top of the other.

6. Move the chop saw back to center and use a piece of scrap wood as a fence to prevent chipping of the finishing edge. Make the cut.

7. Stack again and make the final cut.

8. Place a small line of glue on the base back edge.

9. Use the brad gun to attach to the back, placing 1 brad on each end first and then 3 more along the center. You do not need to let the glue dry before attaching with the brads.

10. Place a small line of glue on the two cut edges, and place the diagonal piece in position.

11. Use the brad gun to attach to the base and back. Repeat on the other side.

12. Measure
1 ½" (40mm) down and
to the center of the
board. Use ⅜ speed
bit to create the hole
for hanging.

13. Repeat the
process for the second
sconce. Finish as
you like!

Photo Credits

All photographs are by Diane Fitzberger except for the following from shutterstock.com:

page 1: sarawuth wannasathit; **page 2:** Thaisucculents; **pages 4/5 and page borders throughout:** POPimage

Index

Note: Page numbers in *italics* indicate projects.